Sun Tzu's
The Art
of War
for Lawyers

Troy Doucet, Esq.

CONTENTS

INTRODUCTION

The Art of War is a book about wisdom, careful planning, and understanding. It teaches the reader a great deal about the nature of people, conflict, and reactions to events in their environment.

Contrary to some people's belief, it is not a book about brutality, bloodiness, or destruction. It does not advocate back-stabbing, unprofessionalism, or rudeness. If anything, it subtly shows you that kind of behavior will lead to ruin. Mastering the Art of War is about mastering calmness and careful analysis, not cruelty.

This book analogizes Sun Tzu's original 2,500 year old text to the practice of law, with a focus on understanding the movements of people, the courts, and opposing parties. In reading it, you should not read it with an eye towards annihilating your opponent, but rather with an eye towards absorbing the material and gaining wisdom. The wisdom in the Art of War unfolds over time as it is digested.

Finally, it is the author's hope that the wisdom in this book be put to good use helping those in need and those facing hardships in their lives. Serving the poor is one of the highest forms of our profession, and the best use of this book is in furthering that effort.

1

LAYING PLANS

Sun Tzu said:

1. The art of war is of vital importance to the State. It is a matter of life and death, a road either to safety or to ruin. Hence it is a subject of inquiry which can on no account be neglected.

2. The art of war, then, is governed by five constant factors, to be taken into account in one's deliberations, when seeking to determine the conditions in the field. These are:

> *(1) The Moral Law;*
>
> *(2) Heaven;*
>
> *(3) Earth;*
>
> *(4) The Commander;*
>
> *(5) Method and Discipline.*

<u>As applied to litigation</u>:

1. Litigation is of vital importance to your client. It is a mechanism that can protect your client's interests, or lead to financial ruin. For this reason, you should carefully study the art of litigation and master how to employ it.

2. Litigation is governed by dynamics that are similar to warfare, in that certain factors must be taken into account when considering whether, and how, to proceed with a matter. Your analysis of these factors will provide you an idea of how you should proceed. They are:

(1) The <u>Justness of the Cause</u> and the appearance of fairness in the outcome sought;

(2) The <u>Court</u>, judge, and law clerk assigned to the case, as well as the jury pool;

(3) The <u>Facts of the Case</u>, the client, opposing party, and applicable laws;

(4) The <u>Attorneys</u> in charge, including their ability and resources; and

(5) The <u>Systems and Discipline</u> in place to ensure the path laid is the path followed.

3. The Moral Law causes the people to be in complete accord with their ruler, so that they will follow him regardless of their lives, undismayed by any danger.

4. Heaven signifies night and day, cold and heat, times and seasons.

5. Earth comprises distances, great and small; danger and security; open ground and narrow passes; the chances of life and death.

6. The Commander stands for the virtues of wisdom, sincerity, benevolence, courage and strictness.

3. The <u>Justness of the Cause</u> means the client's position is consistent with an idea of fairness and justice. When considering whether the client's position is just, look to the ultimate outcome you seek, and evaluate whether that outcome has the feel of righteousness. An outcome that appears just and fair will make ruling in your favor more likely, even if it violates a technical code.

4. The <u>Court</u> signifies the forum in which you will engage your adversary.

Just as a commander can choose to fight in the summer versus winter, you may have a choice of which jurisdiction to sue in. However, once you have engaged in litigation in the forum, the Court is something you may have little control over, but affects your case nonetheless.

5. The <u>Facts of the Case</u> comprise all the evidence in the matter, the client and the client's likeability, and the opposing party and its likeability. It is also comprised of the causes of action that will be at issue, the defenses raised, the law surrounding each, and the rules of procedure.

6. The <u>Attorney</u> in charge means whether the leader of the legal team is wise, sincere, benevolent, tenacious, courageous, and disciplined. He or she has a good reputation and is professional in all dealings.

7. By Method and Discipline are to be understood the marshaling of the army in its proper subdivisions, the graduations of rank amount the officers, the maintenance of roads by which supplies may reach the army, and the control of military expenditure.

8. These five factors should be familiar to every general; he who knows them will be victorious; he who does not know them will fail.

7. The <u>Systems and Discipline</u> means the strength of the legal team supporting the case, and whether the team acts with coherence, efficiency, and with sufficient resources to fight the matter. It also signifies the perseverance of the case despite short term losses, as well as the discipline to continue the strong path that has been laid.

8. These five factors determine the outcome of any case. The attorney who knows the factors and understands their application will be victorious, whereas the attorney who does not know or understand their application will fail.

9. Therefore, in your deliberations, when seeking to determine the military conditions, compare the factors wisely, in this way:

(1) Which of the two sovereigns is imbued with the Moral Law?

(2) Which of the two generals has most ability?

(3) With whom lie the advantages derived from Heaven and Earth?

(4) On which side is Discipline most rigorously enforced?

(5) Which army is stronger?

(6) On which side are officers and men more highly trained?

(7) In which army is there the greater constancy both in reward and punishment?

10. By means of these seven considerations I can forecast victory or defeat.

11. The general that hearkens to my counsel and acts upon it will conquer: Let such a one be retained in command! The general that hearkens not to my counsel nor acts upon it will suffer defeat: - Let such a one be dismissed!

9. Therefore, you must carefully and wisely compare the factors in your matter to determine how you should approach litigation, and under what conditions your client can win. Consider the factors this way:

(1) Which of the parties has the appearance of justice and fairness on their side, and which side will find it easier to sway the judge or jury?

(2) Which side has a more capable attorney leading their team?

(3) Which side does the court tend to support? Which side do the facts better support? Also, which party is more likeable or sympathetic?

(4) Which legal team is more disciplined; which acts more coherently?

(5) Which party has greater resources, strength, stamina, and willingness to stand on principal?

(6) Which legal team has more able and knowledgeable attorneys and staff?

(7) Which team better cultivates their attorneys and staff with rewards and punishments?

10. These seven areas of consideration enable you to predict the outcome of any case.

11. The litigation attorney who listens to the advice given here and acts upon it will win cases, and should remain in command of the client's matter. The attorney who does not listen or disregards this advice will suffer defeat and should be replaced.

12. While heeding the profit of my counsel, avail yourself also of any helpful circumstances over and beyond the ordinary rules.

13. According as circumstances are favorable, one should modify one's plans.

14. All warfare is based on deception.

12. Pay attention to the factors and the advice given here when planning for litigation, but also consider taking advantage of any other favorable circumstance that are present or become evident to you in the matter.

13. Develop a strategic plan based on your client's objectives before entering litigation, but change the plan as necessary to maximize the benefits of new circumstances.

14. All warfare is based on deception.

Litigation encompasses the factors discussed above. How those factors are utilized, manipulated, and employed is a matter of perception over reality. In this sense, each side attempts to develop the presentation of the case in a manner they believe best suits their position. The "reality" that exists may be one thing, but the presentation of that reality is another. The manipulation of this presentation could be called the "deception" on which litigation is based.

15. Hence, when able to attack, we must seem unable; when using our forces, we must seem inactive; when we are near, we must make the enemy believe we are far away; when far away, we must make him believe we are near.

16. Hold out baits to entice the enemy. Feign disorder, and crush him.

15. Therefore, use misdirection as needed to meet the client's objectives. This means gain advantage through the manner in which reality is presented.

For example, if your case is strong and they will not settle, allow them to think you are overworked or lazy to avoid them putting much work into their case. Similarly, if you do not want to delay the case, then ask little of them so it may appear as if you would rather settle than try the case. If you need to settle but your case is weak, bombard them with work and discovery to allow them to think you are preparing for extended litigation. If you want to delay, but cannot afford to expend resources, pick a small issue to fight about and make it a mountain that consumes their time, avoiding other work until the issue is resolved (and using the issue as your excuse for the delay).

This means you should not always show strength, but rather suggests sometimes you should consider demonstrating weakness.

16. Use arguments, evidence, or other issues to entice your opponent into a particular position that is favorable to you. Appear disordered in your argument or position to trigger confusion, and then use that confusion to win the issue.

For example, address one aspect of an issue in a motion that you expect will elicit a particular response, but use your reply to make the winning point.

17. If he is secure at all points, be prepared for him. If he is superior strength, evade him.

18. If your opponent is of choleric temper, seek to irritate him. Pretend to be weak, so he will grow arrogant.

19. If he is taking his ease, give him no rest. If his forces are united, separate them.

17. If the opposing party has good arguments against your good arguments, then you must prepare for litigation. If the opposing party has a winning case, then avoid litigation. If you cannot avoid litigation, then evade their ability to obtain damaging evidence.

18. If your opponent is angry, aggressive, or overly competitive (Type-A personality), then irritate him. He will become reactionary. Further, pretend to be weak so he will grow arrogant and overconfident.

By acting this way, your opponent's energy will be directed towards opposing whatever position you take. When this happens, you can lead him into the position that you have pre-selected for him – the position that serves your goals.

19. If your opponent is overworked or is slowly engaging the litigation, then keep him busy with work, discovery, and motion practice.

If the opposing parties or their counsel are united, then separate them. Create situations that cause internal conflict and disorder. For example, create conflicts of interests between the co-party opponents by raising claims that require they apportion liability among themselves. Alternatively, create conflicts that force each party to engage their own counsel, or turn their witnesses hostile so that the witness assists your case.

20. Attack him where he is unprepared, appear where you are not expected.

21. These military devices, leading to victory, must not be divulged beforehand.

22. Now the general who wins a battle makes many calculations in his temple where the battle is fought. The general who loses a battle makes but few calculations beforehand. Thus do many calculations which leads to victory, and few calculations to defeat. It is by attention to this point that I can foresee who is likely to win or lose.

20. Attack the opposing party where they are not prepared or where they do not expect.

21. Whatever your strategy, do not divulge it before litigation begins. If you litigate against an opponent and use a strategy that plays on his personal weaknesses, never disclose your strategy to him. Any awareness of your strategy will enable your opponent to avoid it.

22. The winning party is the one who carefully considers the factors mentioned above, meticulously calculates a path to victory, and plans the expected course of litigation before engaging in it. The losing party will be the one who engages in litigation without considering the costs or benefits, nor has thought of a complete strategy. This is so important that the winner of the case can be predicted by looking at which has more carefully studied the factors and engaged in strategic planning.

2

WAGING WAR

Sun Tzu said:

1. In the operations of war, where there are in the field a thousand swift chariots, as many heavy chariots, and a hundred thousand mail-clad soldiers, with provisions enough to carry them a thousand half-kilometers, the expenditure at home and at the front, including entertainment of guests, small items such as glue and paint, and sums spent on chariots and armor, will reach the total of a thousand ounces of silver per day. Such is the cost of raising an army of 100,000 men.

2. When you engage in actual fighting, if victory is long in coming, the men's weapons will grow dull and their ardor will be dampened.

3. If you lay siege to a town, you will exhaust your strength.

<u>As to litigation</u>:

1. The costs of litigation must be calculated carefully before engaging in any lawsuit, as well as discussed with the client. The costs can be, and should be, quantified based on the law firm engaged, the complexity of the matter, the witnesses needed, the planned duration of the case, and the evidence involved. The financial toll of litigation will be substantial, and the ongoing cost must be carefully considered by the client prior to filing or answering the lawsuit.

2. Litigation that continues for a long period of time will cause the teams to become tired of the conflict. Their passion for the case will diminish, as will their attention to the details of the matter.

3. If your litigation targets the heart of how the opposing party conducts business, then you will expend considerable energy during litigation and exhaust your strength. This applies also to litigation that would cause the opposing party to close or fundamentally change the operation of a key factory or office.

4. Again, if the campaign is protracted, the resources of the State will not be equal to the strain.

5. Now, when your weapons are dulled, your ardor damped, your strength exhausted and your treasure spent, other chieftains will spring up to take advantage of your extremity. Then no man, however wise, will be able to avert the consequences that must ensue.

4. If litigation continues for a very long time, then the strain it places on the parties will be greater than the resources required to continue it.

5. Once the client or the opponent has engaged in enough litigation that the attorneys are tired, the client's strength exhausted, and the costs sufficiently excessive, others will step in to take advantage of their weakened state.

These repercussions are not limited to one party.   The plaintiff may face MDL challenges from other plaintiffs, face defendants in other cases becoming obstinate at the sign of a weakness, or need to co-counsel with other firms where once not necessary. The defense could face multiple other lawsuits, greater negative publicity, and the potential for criminal investigations.

No client or leader, however wise, will be able to avoid negative consequences from a protracted case. There is no limitation to these consequences, such that they could arise in any number of unforeseen ways.

6. Thus, though we have heard of stupid haste in war, cleverness has never been seen associated with long delays.

7. There is no instance of a country having benefited from prolonged warfare.

8. It is only one who is thoroughly acquainted with the evils of war that can thoroughly understand the profitable way of carrying it on.

9. The skillful solider does not raise a second levy, neither are his supply-wagons loaded more than twice.

10. Bring war material with you from home, but forage food from the enemy. Thus the army will have food enough for its needs.

6. We all know of stupid haste during litigation, but we rarely hear of protracted litigation being associated with cleverness.

7. While some might view protracted litigation as helpful to a defendant, the weakened state, stress, and finances of the parties after protracted litigation means there is no long-term benefit for either side.

8. Only an individual who is thoroughly acquainted with the toll that litigation takes on all involved can understand the way to profitably engage in it.

9. The skillful litigator does not make the same mistake twice, instead getting the work done correctly the first time.

For example, the time and energy in responding to a motion to dismiss for failing to include a necessary element of a claim is excessively more costly than simply researching the claim before drafting and ensuring all the elements are well pled.

10. As much as possible, work with claims or defenses that allow for fee-shifting of attorney's fees and costs, so that your efforts are paid for by the opposing party. Also, file the suit with the evidence you have, but acquire evidence and other information from your opponent. Thus, you will have profits to survive on.

11. Poverty of the State exchequer causes an army to be maintained by contributions from a distance. Contributing to maintain an army at a distance causes the people to be impoverished.

12. On the other hand, the proximity of an army causes prices to go up; and high prices cause the people's substance to be drained away. When their substance is drained away, the peasantry will be afflicted by heavy exactions.

13. When the spirit is destroyed and resources are gone, the partner's wealth will be considerably affected.

14. With this loss of substance and exhaustion of strength, the homes of the people will be stripped bare, and three-tenths of their income will be dissipated; while government expenses for broken chariots, worn-out horses, breast-plates and helmets, bows and arrows, spears and shields, protective mantles, draught-oxen and heavy wagons, will amount to four-tenths of its total revenue.

11. Beyond the fact that lengthy litigation costs more, the cost of physical proximity of the counsel, evidence, and the court also contribute towards draining the financial resources of the party.

The greater the distance the attorney, clients, or evidence must travel, then the more costly the litigation. With greater distances comes a greater likelihood the client will become impoverished. Thus, to save costs, stay as local as possible.

12. On the other hand, when litigation is close by, it will have a draining effect on the client's staff and organization. If stressors and negative publicity are geographically near, then productivity will decrease and business will suffer.

13. When the client's spirit is destroyed by the fight, and its disposable funds completely spent on the litigation, the client's long-term viability will be considerably affected.

14. At that point, the quality and quantity of produced goods and services produced by the client will suffer, its income will decrease, and a greater percentage of the client's income will be devoted to the litigation. Further, the client's staff will suffer by having fewer raises, perks, and improvements at the office.

15. Hence a wise general makes a point of foraging on the enemy. One cartload of the enemy's provisions is equivalent to twenty of one's own, and likewise a single pound of his material is equivalent to twenty from one's own store.

16. Therefore in chariot fighting, when ten or more chariots have been taken, those should be rewarded who took the first. Our own flags should be substituted for those of the enemy, and the chariots mingled and used in conjunction with ours.

15. Hence, a wise attorney structures a lawsuit to avoid travel, costs, and expenses. The wise attorney also raises claims where evidence is easily ascertainable, and attempts to use fee shifting provisions to secure payment from the opposing party. Using these cost savings methods substantially decreases the burden to his client.

16. Where you are able to acquire payment from the opposing party for fees or costs, the associate attorney who successfully argued for that payment should be rewarded the most for the job well done. Then, a bonus should be paid to the team, so that everyone values the associate's success rather than being resentful of it.

17. The captured soldiers should be kindly treated and kept.

18. This is called using the conquered foe to augment one's one strength.

19. Thus it may be known that the leader of armies is the arbiter of the people's fate, the man on whom it depends whether the nation shall be in peace or in peril.

17. You should always treat the losing opponent and counsel with respect and professionalism.

18. This is called using the conquered foe to augment your strength.

While litigation can become contentious, by showing respect for the losing opponent after the battle is done, you add to the strength of your leadership and position. This is especially true in the legal profession, where extending respect to the losing opponent gains not only the respect of your associates, but the colleagues who you will frequently interact with over the course of your career. It also shows your moral character and contributes to the factors described in chapter one, *Laying Plans*, which will contribute to further wins in other cases.

19.As the lead attorney, you hold the fate of your client in the balance. You are the one who your client depends on to determine whether he will be at peace or face litigation. Remember this.

3

ATTACK BY STRATAGEM

Sun Tzu said:

1. *In the practical art of war, the best thing of all is to take the enemy's country whole and intact; to shatter and destroy it is not so good. So, too, it is better to recapture an army entire than to destroy it, to capture a regiment, a detachment or a company entire than to destroy them.*

2. *Hence to fight and conquer in all your battles is not supreme excellence; supreme excellence consists of breaking the enemy's resistance without fighting.*

As to litigation:

1. The best outcome is resolving a case without having to engage in litigation. A pre-lawsuit settlement favorably resolves the matter for all involved at minimal cost, and sometimes minimal effort.

Pursuing litigation that results in the destruction of the opponent is not favorable. It requires substantial cost, energy, and effort, and may result in the closure or bankruptcy of your opponent.

2. Consistently winning cases through litigation requires expending energy and cost on the effort, which is not the pinnacle of excellence. The greatest level of achievement is securing a favorable settlement or outcome before litigation ever begins. Winning at all costs is simply not as favorable as winning at no (or minimal) costs.

(With litigation, keep in mind that a favorable outcome does not necessarily mean a complete victory through the litigation process. The most important outcome is one that matches the client's objectives. If you are able to meet the client's objectives, then the matter has been successfully pursued.)

3. Thus the highest form of generalship is to balk the enemy's plans; the next best is to prevent the junction of the enemy's forces; then next in order is to attack the enemy's army in the field; and the worst policy of all is to besiege walled cities.

3. The highest form of resolving litigation is to attack the opponent's legal or factual position before the matter is filed. This can include addressing their claims or defenses directly, citing to case law or contrary factual information that demonstrates opposition is futile.

The next highest form of resolving litigation in your favor is to divide the opposing parties, or prevent them from coming together as a joint force.

This can be done, for example, by drafting the complaint or answer in such a way that creates a conflict between otherwise joint adversaries. It can also be accomplished through dividing their claims or attacking a fragment of a legal element.

Next best is to use tactics that intimidate the opposing party or its counsel with work or claims, possibly by co-counseling with a large or reputable law firm.

Worst is to engage the opponent in litigation, especially if the matter will alter or eliminate its core business practice.

4. The rule is, not be besiege walled cities if it can possibly be avoided. The preparation of mantles, movable shelters, and various implement of war, will take up three whole months; and the piling up of mounds against the walls will take three months more.

5. The general, unable to control his irritation, will launch his men to the assault like swarming ants, with the result that one-third of his men are slain, while the town still remains untaken. Such are the disastrous effects of a siege.

6. Therefore the skillful leader subdues the enemy's troops without any fighting; he captures their cities without laying siege to them; he overthrows their kingdom without lengthy operations in the field.

4. Do not attack an opponent's core business if it can be avoided. The preparation to properly understand its core business (with all of its nuances) as you prepare for litigation will take considerable time. Finding viable causes of action and defenses will take considerable more, especially if the opponent views their core business as legitimate.

This goes directly to the costs of the matter and recognizing that the more important the matter is to your opponent, the more time, energy, and costs you will expend simply preparing for the lawsuit.

5. The attorney who becomes irritated enough by the opposing party to attack its core business directly will expend considerable time, energy, and resources such that his client's coffers will be greatly diminished well before the litigation is complete. Such are the disastrous effects of a frontal attack on an opponent's core business.

6. Therefore, the most skilled litigator successfully settles a case before ever filing a lawsuit. He secures the award with absolute minimal conflict, preserving his and his client's resources, and even the opponent's resources.

7. With his forces intact he will become the master of the Empire, and thus, without losing a man, his triumph will be complete.

8. This is the method of attacking by stratagem.

9. It is the rule in war, if our forces are ten to the enemy's one, then surround him; if five to one, attack him; if twice as numerous, to divide our army into two.

10. If equally matched, we can offer battle; if slightly inferior in numbers, we can avoid the enemy; if quite unequal in every way, we can flee from him.

7. By winning a case before ever filing it, this skilled litigator will be hailed as a master of litigation, with the pinnacle of the triumph stemming from conserving his own firm's resources.

8. Winning without litigation is accomplished through employing strategy.

9. If your client's resources are ten times its opponents, then demonstrate the resource differential by putting many names on the pleading, employing large co-counsel, and drafting lengthy and detailed initial briefings. Use the litigation tools at your disposal to overwhelm your opponent or its counsel.

If your client's resources are five to one, then file suit against the opposing party and demonstrate by resource differential when possible so that they may understand they are outmatched.

If your client's resources are two to one, then you may want to consider limiting your causes of action or defenses to limit the breadth of discovery and to make the case more manageable. This may also mean limiting the litigation to utilize less staff.

10. If the parties are equally matched, they may decide to engage in battle. If your client's resources are slightly inferior, then you can attempt to avoid litigation or settle early. If your client's resources are significantly inferior, litigation should be avoided.

11. Hence, though an obstinate fight may be made by a small force, in the end it must be captured by the larger force.

12. Now the general is the bulwark of the State; if the bulwark is complete at all points, the State will be strong; if the bulwark is defective, the State will be weak.

13. There are three ways in which a ruler can bring misfortune upon his army: -

(1) By commanding the army to advance or to retreat, being ignorant to the fact that it cannot obey. This is called hobbling the army.

(2) By attempting to govern an army in the same way as he administers a kingdom, being ignorant of the conditions which exist in an army. This causes restlessness in the soldier's minds.

(3) By employing the officers of his army without discrimination, through ignorance of the military principle of adaptation to circumstances. This shakes the confidence of the solders.

11. While a client with inferior resources may want to litigate to the bitter end against a organization with more resources, it will eventually lead to the opposing party having the case resolved on its terms.

12. The attorney leading the litigation must be strong, talented, hardworking, and benevolent when leading the team. If the lead attorney is these things, then the client's objectives will be well protected. Otherwise, the client's position will be weak and subject to loss.

13. There are three ways in which the lead attorney can bring misfortune on his legal team:

(1) By taking some action within the litigation while being ignorant that the rules, process, or deadlines prohibit that action. This is called hobbling the team.

(2) By attempting to employ business or management logic to the litigation team, being ignorant of the varying roles that the team members play. This causes incoherence, and restlessness in the team members' minds.

(3) By indiscriminately employing team members in roles that they do not belong, especially inappropriate appointments to leadership positions. This shakes the team's confidence.

14. But when the army is restless and distrustful, trouble is sure to come from the other feudal princes. This is simply bringing anarchy into the army, and flinging victory away.

15. Thus we may know that there are five essentials for victory:

(1) He will win who knows when to fight and when not to fight.

(2) He will win who knows how to handle both superior and inferior forces.

(3) He will win whose army is animated by the same spirit throughout all its ranks.

(4) He will win who, prepared himself, waits to take the enemy unprepared.

(5) He will win who has military capacity and is not interfered with by the sovereign.

16. Hence the saying: If you know the enemy and know yourself, you need not fear the result of a hundred battles. If you know yourself but not the enemy, for every victory gained you will also suffer a defeat. If you know neither the enemy nor yourself, you will succumb in every battle.

14. When the litigation team becomes confused, frustrated, or in conflict due to poor leadership by the lead attorney, then other high-ranked team attorneys will seek to wrestle away control. This will lead to greater internal conflict and will negatively impact the prospect of victory.

15. There are five essential things necessary for a winning strategy:

(1) Knowing when to fight and when not to fight.

(2) Knowing how to work with limited resources when necessary, and how to employ large resources when available.

(3) Having a legal team that shares the same spirit as its leader.

(4) Remaining prepared, with the patience to wait until the opponent is unprepared to act.

(5) Having great litigation ability and a client that does not micromanage the case.

16. As said by Sun Tzu:

If you know the enemy and know yourself, you need not fear the result of a hundred battles. If you know yourself but not the enemy, for every victory gained you will also suffer a defeat. If you know neither the enemy nor yourself, you will succumb in every battle.

4
TACTICAL DISPOSITIONS

Sun Tzu said:

1. The good fighters of old first put themselves beyond the possibility of defeat, and then waited for an opportunity of defeating the enemy.

2. To secure ourselves against defeat lies in our own hands, but the opportunity of defeating the enemy is provided by the enemy himself.

3. Thus the good fighter is able to secure himself against defeat, but cannot make certain of defeating the enemy.

4. Hence the saying: One may know how to conquer without being able to do it.

5. Security against defeat implies defensive tactics; ability to defeat the enemy means taking the offensive.

1. An experienced litigator will first realize the events necessary for his position to be victorious, and then wait for those events to occur before acting.

2. Your ability to secure your position *against defeat* lies in your own hands. The preparation, research, and energy you put into understanding your position, and properly prosecuting it, determines whether your opponent has an opportunity to defeat you. Similarly, the opportunities you have to defeat your opponent will become available through the actions of your opponent; your opponent will create the opportunities for you to beat them.

3. Thus, the good lawyer is able to prepare his defensive position well, but a good defense does not mean a good offense. In other words, you can secure the strength of your own position because you have control over it, but cannot secure the weakness of your opponent because that is under the control of your opponent.

4. This means that you may know how to beat your opponent, but if he has not opened that door for you, then you cannot walk through it.

5. Securing your position against defeat implies using defensive tactics. Being able to defeat your opponent utilizes offensive tactics.

6. *Standing on the defensive indicates sufficient strength; attacking, a superabundance of strength.*

7. *The general who is skilled in defense hides in the most secret recesses of the earth; he who is skilled in attack flashes forth from the upmost heights of heaven. Thus on the one hand we have the ability to protect ourselves; on the other, a victory that is complete.*

8. *The better of the two will obtain victory.*

9. *To see victory only when it is within the kin of the common herd is not the acme of excellence.*

10. *Neither is it the acme of excellence if you fight and conquer and the whole Empire says: "Well done!"*

6. Holding a winning defensive position requires sufficient strength, but attacking requires an abundance of it. Consider the defendant who can obstruct discovery, versus the plaintiff who needs to hunt it down from multiple sources.

7. An attorney who is skilled at defense layers his work in technicalities, objections, and legalities. An attorney who is skilled in the attack moves quickly to uncover the facts and present the merits.

8. The better of the two will win.

9. If you bring or defend cases that already have a worn path to your victory, then this is not the pinnacle of litigation excellence. This is evident in those lawyers that avoid taking cases because they risk loss, rather than those attorneys that take risky cases and execute a path to victory.

10. The platitudes received upon winning are equally not signs of excellence in litigation. Notes of congratulations do not mean an attorney is great, only that he or she is receiving a note of congratulation.

11. To lift an autumn leaf is no sign of great strength; to see the sun and moon are no sign of sharp sight; to hear the noise of thunder is no sign of a quick ear.

12. What the ancients called a clever fighter is one who not only wins, but excels in winning with ease.

13. Hence his victories bring him neither reputation for wisdom nor credit for courage.

14. He wins his battles by making no mistakes.

15. Making no mistakes is what establishes the certainty of victory, for it means conquering an enemy that is already defeated.

11. As stated: To lift an autumn leaf is not a sign of great strength. To see the sun and moon is not a sign of sharp sight. To hear the noise of thunder is not a sign of a quick ear.

Obtaining excellence in litigation is about understanding the nature of litigation, and of its subtleties. Litigation excellence is not found in winning cases that everyone wins, but in understanding it in such a way that you can see victory in cases others may avoid, whether or not you opt to pursue them.

12. A clever litigator not only wins, but excels in winning with ease.

13.An attorney who excels at litigation is seen as a natural at it, someone *expected* to win. This is such that his victories no longer build upon his reputation or garner him greater credit for courage.

14. This attorney wins by not making mistakes, either defensively or offensively. This attorney has the wisdom and foresight to ensure no mistakes are made.

15. Making no mistakes ensures victory because it means that the litigation walked the path that you designed for it. Since no mistakes were made, your path to victory was realized.

16. Hence the skillful fighter puts himself into a position which makes defeat impossible, and does not miss the moment for defeating the enemy.

17. Thus it is that in war that victorious strategist only seeks battle after the victory has been won, whereas he who is destined to defeat first fights and afterward looks for victory.

18. The consummate leader cultivates the Moral Law, and strictly adheres to method and discipline; thus it is in his power to control success.

19. In respect to military method, we have, firstly, Measurement; secondly, Estimation of quantity; thirdly, Calculation; fourthly, Balancing of chances; fifthly, Victory.

16. Thus, the skillful attorney moves his client into the position that makes defeat impossible, and then waits for the moment to defeat his opponent.

17. The victorious attorney only engages in litigation after he has planned a path to victory. The attorney destined to fail first enters into litigation and then only afterwards looks for victory.

18. The wise litigator develops the case so that they appear to show the justness of the cause is on the side of his client, and methodically approaches the litigation with method and disciple. These two factors (justness and strategic ability) impact the third factor (facts of the case) and the fourth factor (attorneys in charge). Thus, by controlling just two factors - the appearance of justness and the application of discipline - the attorney has the power to control success.

19. In respect to the fifth factor of (Systems and Discipline), consider what resources are available and what resources are necessary to win, then calculate the possible outcomes, balance of likelihoods of those outcomes, and finally consider whether you will obtain victory (meeting the client's objectives).

20. Measurement owes its existence to Earth; Estimation of quantity to Measurement; Calculation to Estimation of quantity; Balancing of chances to Calculation; and Victory to Balancing of chances.

21. A victorious army opposed to a routed one, is as a pound's weight placed in the scale against a single grain.

22. The onrush of a conquering force is like the bursting of pent-up waters into a chasm a thousand fathoms deep.

20. You must look at the Facts of the case to determine what resources are available to you. Then, you can determine what resources are still needed to win. Once you know what resources you have and what resources are needed to win, you can determine possible outcomes and weigh the likelihood of those outcomes. At that point, you will be able to determine whether you are able to reach the client's objectives.

21. There is very little comparison between winning and losing a case. The winner's victory is everything compared to the complete cost to the loser.

22. The victor pursues his winning course with considerable strength, as he is merely executing the path to victory that has already been set.

5
ENERGY

Sun Tzu said:

1. The control of large force is the same principle as the control of a few men: It is merely a question of dividing up their numbers.

2. Fighting with a large army under your command is nowise different from fighting with a small one: It is merely a question of instituting signs and signals.

3. To ensure that your whole host may withstand the brunt of the enemy's attack and remain unshaken – this is affected by maneuvers direct and indirect.

4. That the impact of your army may be a like a grindstone dashed against an egg – this is effected by the science of weak points and strong.

5. In all fighting, the direct method may be used for joining battle, but indirect methods will be needed in order to secure victory.

6. Indirect tactics, efficiently applied, are inexhaustible as Heaven and Earth, unending as the flow of rivers and streams; like the sun and moon, they end but to begin anew; like the four seasons, they pass away to return once more.

1. Control of a large lawsuit or team of lawyers employs the same principle as a small lawsuit or team. Simply divide up the tasks, or compartmentalize teams and people to the manage entire process efficiently.

2. A large staff under your control is just as easily managed as a small one. You just need to effectively communicate with everyone.

3. Withstanding that fact, the challenges of litigation are accomplished through direct and indirect maneuvering in pleading, discovery, motion practice, and trial.

4. Achieving a resounding win requires a holistic and comprehensive use of direct and indirect actions. It requires a complete understanding of the nature of litigation, so that the weak and the strong may be effectively utilized to your advantage.

5. Engaging in pleading, discovery, and motion practice is the direct method of engaging in litigation. However, indirect actions during the litigation (e.g., developing the facts, effecting one of the factors, thinking creatively) is also necessary to win.

6. The indirect methods of engaging in litigation are endless, and are as varying as the facts and procedural posture of the case before you. They are also always available in every case, like the permanence of the sun and moon. Like the passing of the seasons, when methods end in one case, they will again be available in another.

7. *There are not more than five musical notes, yet the combinations of these five give rise to more melodies than can ever be heard. There are not more than five primary colors (blue, yellow, red, white and black), yet in combination they produce more hues than can ever be seen. There are not more than five cardinal tastes (sour, acid, salt, sweet and bitters), yet combinations of them yield more flavors than can ever be tasted.*

8. *In battle, there are not more than two methods of attack — the direct and the indirect; yet these two in combination giver rise to an endless series of maneuvers.*

9. *The direct and the indirect lead on to each other in turn. It is like moving in a circle — you never come to an end. Who can exhaust the possibilities of their combination?*

10. *The onset of troops is like the rush of a torrent which will even roll stones along in its course.*

7. Sun Tzu uses three examples to demonstrate the variances available to you in any situation that may otherwise appear simple. He points out that there are only five primary musical notes, colors (blue, yellow, red, white and black), and human tastes (sour, acid, salt, sweet, and bitter), but so many combinations of each that we could never experience them all.

Similarly, there are only a handful of usual motions in litigation, and only a handful of elements for each individual claim. Yet, there are so many factual scenarios, legal arguments, and procedural tools available in litigation, that the variations for indirect actions are limitless.

8. In litigation, there are only two methods of attack. Those are the direct and indirect. Yet, the variations of their use are limitless, enabling an endless series of maneuvers.

9. Remember that direct actions and indirect actions are used in concert, with one playing into the other. It is about a continual movement, like two ideas moving together, over and under, in a circle that never ends.

10. Filing the lawsuit is like a rush of water in a stream that rolls stones along its course. There is momentum created by the lawsuit's initial filing.

11. The quality decision is like the well-timed swoop of a falcon which enables it to strike and destroy its victim.

12. Therefore the good fighter will be terrible in his onset, and prompt in his decisions.

13. Energy may be likened to the bending of a crossbow; decision, to the releasing of a trigger.

14. Amid the turmoil and tumult of battle, there may be seeming disorder and yet no real disorder at all; amid confusion and chaos, your array may be without head or tail, yet it will be proof against defeat.

11. A quality decision demonstrates precision in time and space, like the swoop of a falcon when it kills its prey.

12. Therefore, the good litigator will file a startling lawsuit, followed by precise and prompt decision making.

13. Energy is accumulated like the bending of a crossbow, with a decision to employ it like the releasing of the trigger.

14. Amid the twists and turns of litigation, there may seem to be disorder, such as in motion practice or discovery. However, this may be an illusion. There may actually be no disorder at all.

Similarly, your staff or the matter may seem to be without a head or tail to the other side, but that may be a matter of planned deception, leading to your win.

15. Simulated disorder postulates perfect discipline, simulated fear postulates courage; simulated weakness postulates strength. Hiding order beneath the cloak of disorder is simply a question of subdivision; concealing courage under a show of timidity presupposes a fund of latent energy; masking strength with weakness is to be effected by tactical dispositions.

16. Thus one who is skilful at keeping the enemy on the move maintains deceitful appearances, according to which the enemy will act. He sacrifices something that the enemy may snatch at it.

17. By holding out baits, he keeps him on the march; then with a body of picked men he lies in wait for him.

18. When he utilizes combined energy, his fighting men become as it were like unto rolling logs or stones. For it is the nature of a log or stone to remain motionless on level ground, and to move when on a slope; if four-cornered, to come to a standstill, but if round-shaped, to go rolling down.

19. Thus the energy developed by good fighting men is as the momentum of a round stone rolled down a mountain thousands of feet in height. So much on the subject of energy.

15. When a strategic plan simulates disorder, this suggests that there is perfect discipline. When a strategic plan simulates fear, this suggests courage.

Simulating disorder is achieved by the subdivision of resources or people.

Concealing courage under a show of timidity requires a reserve of energy to draw from. Masking strength with weakness is accomplished through strategic, tactical movements.

16. Thus, a litigator who is skillful in keeping his opponent chasing irrelevant victories is a one who entices his opponent with leads he knows will be followed. Sometimes this requires sacrificing something as bait.

17. By holding out bait, you can lure your opponent into a preselected position that is beneficial for you to attack.

18. A carefully crafted strategic plan that combines direct and indirection actions enables a litigator to execute it with force and direction. A good plan is like turning a motionless log or stone into a mighty force by pushing it down a hill.

19. Thus, the energy released by the implementation of an excellently crafted plan has the momentum of a round stone rolled down a mountain that is a thousand feet tall.

This concludes the subject of energy.

6
WEAK POINTS AND STRONG

Sun Tzu said:

1. *Whoever is first in the field and awaits the coming of the enemy, will be fresh for the fight; whoever is second in the field and has to hasten the battle will arrive exhausted.*

2. *Therefore the clever combatant imposes his will on the enemy, but does not allow the enemy's will to be imposed on him.*

3. *By holding out advantages to him, has can cause the enemy to approach of his own accord; or, by inflicting damage, he can make it impossible for the enemy to draw near.*

4. *If the enemy is taking his ease, you can harass him; if well supplied with food, you can starve him out; if quietly encamped, you can force him to move.*

5. *Appear at points which the enemy must hasten to defend; march swiftly to places where you are not expected.*

1. Being plaintiff is generally better than being defendant, as you control the introduction of the case, jurisdiction, venue, and filing time. You also have more time to prepare and be fresh for the fight. The opponent who has to hurry will arrive less prepared.

2. Therefore, the clever litigator controls the instigation of a case, causing his opponent to come to him. He does not allow his opponent to determine the terms of the engagement.

3. You can control whether your opponent draws closer or moves further away. By holding out advantages to him, you can cause him to move closer without your prodding. Conversely, you can keep your opponent away by creating conflict or cost in the area you want him to avoid.

4. If your opponent is taking his time with a matter, you can harass him. If he is well supplied with resources, you can drain them with prolonged litigation. If he is quietly waiting, you can force him to move.

5. Engage your opponent on issues that he must hasten to defend.

Engage in arguments or discovery where you are not expected.

6. An army may march great distances without distress, if it marches through country where the enemy is not.

7. You can be sure of succeeding in your attacks if you only attack placed where are undefended. You can ensure the safety of your defense if you only hold positions that cannot be attacked.

8. Hence that general is skillful in attack whose opponent does not know what to defend; and he is skillful in defense whose opponent does not know what to attack.

9. O divine art of subtlety and secrecy! Through you, we learn to be invisible, through you inaudible; and hence we can hold the enemy's fate in our hands.

6. You can acquire considerable evidence when your opponent does not object to its production, and can achieve great strides in the litigation in areas that you are not opposed.

7. You can be sure of success if you only attack issues that are undefended, or cannot be defended. Conversely, you can be sure of your defense when it cannot be attacked.

8. The skillful general hides his planned place of attack from his opponent. Further, his masks his weak points so that his opponent does not know where to attack him.

Here, Sun Tzu takes a different path to showing you how to be successful in a matter. Rather than directly attacking undefended positions (which is implied from the last paragraph), he suggests that the skilled attacker develops a strategy whereby his opponent does not know where the attack will come from.

For example, using subpoenas is a direct action in a case, but sending those subpoenas to multiple contacts and people is using indirect actions to hide your purpose.

9. This kind of maneuvering requires the art of subtlety and secrecy! Mastering this is how to make your goals invisible and inaudible, enabling you to hold your opponent's fate in your hands.

10. You may advance and be absolutely irresistible, if you make for the enemy's weak points; you may retire and be safe from pursuit if your movements are more rapid than those of the enemy.

11. If we wish to fight, the enemy can be forced to an engagement even though he is sheltered behind a high rampart and a deep ditch. All we need do is attack some other place that he will be obliged to relieve.

12. If we do not wish to fight, we can prevent the enemy from engaging us even though the lines of our encampment are merely traced out on the ground. All we need do is to throw something odd and unaccountable in his way.

10. You can control where your opponent goes if you attack his weak points. You can avoid being attacked if your movements are faster than his.

11. If you opponent has a strong line of defense in a particular area, then getting him to move is as easy as attacking some other issue that will require him to divert his time and resources.

For example, if you cannot obtain what you need directly from your opponent, look to third parties whom you can subpoena for the information. His strength resisting discovery is avoided by seeking information elsewhere. Further, this action will cause your opponent's efforts to shift towards someplace other than a direct refusal to provide the evidence.

This lesson also suggests that you could seek discovery in an unrelated area to move your opponent in a new direction. The key here is about moving your opponent away from a point of strength to another place of your choosing.

12. If you would like to avoid confrontation on a particular issue at the moment, you can stall the normal course of events by throwing something odd or unaccountable in your opponent's path.

13. By discovering the enemy's dispositions and remaining invisible ourselves, we can keep our forces concentrated, which the enemy's must be divided.

14. We can form a single united body, while the enemy must split up into fractions. Hence there will be a whole pitted against separate parts of a whole, which means that we shall be many to the enemy's few.

15. And if we are able thus to attack an inferior force with a superior one, our opponents will be in dire straits.

16. The spot where we intend to fight must not be made known; for then the enemy will have to prepare against a possible attack at several different points; and his forces being thus distributed in many directions, the numbers we shall have to face at any given point will be proportionality few.

13. If you can discover how your opponent will be proceeding with the matter while your strategy remains hidden, then you can concentrate your energy, while his must be divided.

14. In this sense, you will be able to concentrate your energy in a single direction while your opponent must think about everywhere you could go. You will be pitting a solid beam of energy against his many smaller fragments. You will be "many," compared to your opponent's "few."

15. If you combine your focused energy against his fragment, and if your force is overall stronger than his, then your opponent truly will be in dire straits.

16. The exact issue where you intend to fight should not be made known, for then your opponent can focus on that particular issue. You should instead cause your opponent to prepare for multiple arguments so that his energy and forces are distributed in many different directions. This way, his argument on any given point will not be as robust as if he could focus all his energy on just one position.

17. For shall the enemy strengthen his front, he will weaken his rear; should he strengthen his rear, he will weaken his front; should he strengthen his right, he will weaken his left. If he sends reinforcements everywhere, he will everywhere be weak.

18. Numerical weakness comes from having to prepare against possible attacks, numerical strength comes from compelling our adversary to make these preparations against us.

19. Knowing the place and the time of the coming battle, we may concentrate from the greatest distances in order to fight.

17. Focusing on one issue will naturally cause less focus to be placed on another. If your opponent focuses more on issue 1, then issue 2 will suffer. Conversely, if resources are spent on issue 2, then less focus will be on issue 1. If your opponent focuses on all the issues equally, then all of the arguments will be weak.

18. As it pertains to preparing for multiple issues, your weakness comes from having to prepare for multiple lines of attack by the other side.

Your strength comes from forcing the other side to prepare for multiple lines of attack by you.

19. The further in advance that you know how the litigation will proceed, the greater your ability to concentrate your efforts.

20. But, if neither time nor place be known, then the left wing will be impotent to support the right, the right equally impotent to support the left, the front unable to relieve the rear, or the rear to support the front. How much more so if the furthest portions of the army are anything under [thirty miles] apart, and even the nearest are separated by [one mile].

21. Though according to my estimate the soldiers of Yueh exceed our own in number, that shall advantage them nothing in the matter of victory. I say then that victory can be achieved.

22. Though the enemy is stronger in numbers, we may prevent him from fighting. Scheme so as to discover his plans and the likelihood of their success.

23. Rouse him, and learn the principle of his activity or inactivity. Force him to reveal himself, so as to find out his vulnerable spots.

20. However, if you do not know how the matter will proceed, you will be faced with a diminished ability to shift gears or provide support to the areas of the fight that need it. The further apart the issues that you have to attack, the more difficult it will be for you to provide support for the ones that need it.

For example, consider deadlines in litigation and how you can lose evidentiary development when you are forced to chase other evidence that will not ultimately be at issue in the case. When your resources are centered in one area, but another area becomes the subject of the litigation, your energy and ability to attack and defend the new area is diminished. This occurs if you do not know in advance how the matter will proceed.

21. Being outnumbered does not mean you will lose. You can still prevail.

22. Even if your opponent is stronger in numbers or resources, you can prevent him from fighting. Try to discover what his strategy is going to be in order to estimate his likelihood of success.

23. Communicate with opposing counsel (or unrepresented party) to determine their position and how they plan to proceed. Force your opponent to reveal his intentions to discover his vulnerable spots.

24. Carefully compare the opposing army with your own, so that you may know where strength is super abundant and where it is deficient.

25. In making tactical dispositions, the highest pitch you can attain is to conceal them; conceal your dispositions, and you will be sage from the prying of the subtlest spies, from the machinations of the wisest brains.

26. How victory may be produced for them out of the enemy's own tactics – that is what the multitude cannot comprehend.

27. All men can see the tactics whereby I conquer, but what none can see is the strategy out of which victory is evolved.

28. Do not repeat the tactics which have gained you one victory, but let your methods be regulated by the infinite variety of circumstances.

29. Military tactics are like unto water; for water in its natural course runs away from high places and hastens downwards.

30. So in war, the way is to avoid what is strong and to strike at what is weak.

31. Water shapes its course according to the nature of the ground over which it flows; the solider works out his victory in relation to the foe that he is facing.

24. Compare both sides and determine where each side's strengths and weaknesses lie.

25. The highest level of applying strategy is to conceal your movements from even the wisest strategists.

26. You can obtain a victory using your opponent's own tactics to his disadvantage. However, accomplishing this is something that few people have the ability to do, let alone comprehend.

27. After the litigation is over, everyone can analyze the tactics that you used to obtain the victory. However, they will not be able to see the strategy as it was employed.

28. Do not repeat tactics that you have used once before to win, but rather change your methods and arguments based on the new set of facts before you.

29. Like with water, you should avoid wading into areas that present danger for you, and instead focus on the areas that are safe.

30. So when fighting a lawsuit, avoid the points that are strong for your opponent and focus on those points where your opponent is weak.

31. You will face areas of strength and areas of weakness. Your victory comes from understanding where those areas lie and planning your strategy around them.

32. Therefore, just as water retains no constant shape, so in warfare there are no constant conditions.

33. He, who can modify his tactics in relation to his opponent and thereby succeed in winning, may be called a heaven-born captain.

34. The five elements (water, fire, wood, metal, earth) are not always equally predominant; the four seasons make way for each other in turn. There are short days and long; the moon has its periods of waning and waxing.

32. Just as flowing water retains no constant shape, so too are the variations and changes that you will face in one matter that are different from the last.

33. The attorney who wins a case because of an ability to modify tactics based on the facts, and his opponent, is a "heaven-born" litigator.

34. Like the variations in changing seasons and changing length in days, the facts and tactics in each case must be different, with some elements or claims sometimes taking prominence over others.

7
MANUEVERING

Sun Tzu said:

1. In war, the general receives his commands from the sovereign.

2. Having to collect an army and concentrated his forces, he must blend and harmonize the different elements thereof before pitching his camp.

3. After that, comes tactical maneuvering, than which there is nothing more difficult. The difficulty of tactical maneuvering consists in turning the devious into the direct, and misfortune into gain.

4. Thus, to take a long and circuitous route, after enticing the enemy out of the way and though starting after he, to contrive to reach the goal before him, shows knowledge of the artifice of deviation.

5. Maneuvering with an army is advantageous; with an undisciplined multitude, most dangerous.

6. If you set a fully equipped army in march in order to snatch an advantage, the chances are that you will be too late. On the other hand, to detach a flying column for the purpose involves the sacrifice of its baggage and stores.

1. In litigation, the attorney receives his commands from the client.

2. Once directed to begin litigation, the attorney must bring together the evidence, facts, causes of actions, defenses, people, and resources into a strategic plan.

3. After the plan is established, he must implement the plan, which is more difficult. Implementing the plan consists of organizing the scattered into the direct, and turning misfortune into gain.

4. In implanting the plan, the skillful attorney can cause his opponent to follow him around winding paths before reaching the destination pre-set by the skillful attorney.

5. It is better to enter litigation when your team is trained and skilled. If your team is neither, then entering into litigation is dangerous.

6. If you turn your entire organization towards pursuing a new opportunity before it, the chances are you will be too late to capitalize on that opportunity. However, you can direct a few skilled members of your team to undertake the opportunity, but that may involve some sacrifice of resources or quality to achieve.

7. Thus, if you order your men to roll up their buff-coats, and make forced marches without halting day or night, covering double the usual distance at a stretch, doing a hundred li in order to wrest an advantage, the leaders of all your three divisions will fall into the hands of the enemy.

8. The stronger men will be in front; the jaded ones will fall behind, and on this plan only one-tenth of your army will reach its destination.

9. If you march fifty li in order to out maneuver the enemy, you will lose the leader of your first division, and only half your force will reach the goal. If you march thirty li with the same object, two-thirds of your army will arrive.

10. We may take it then that an army without its baggage-train is lost; without provisions it is lost; without bases of supply it is lost.

7. If you turn your entire organization to quickly pursuing an opportunity without the proper resources, you will suffer the loss of the opportunity.

8. This will be because your strongest staff will be in the front, but the weaker ones unable to follow, leading to only a tenth of your staff being able to effectively pursue the goal.

9. The further you must go and the more resources needed to capitalize on the opportunity, the less likely you will be to acquire it.

10. If your entire organization is needed to capitalize on an opportunity, but you cannot deploy all of the organization's resources at the same time then, simply put, you will incur loss. You cannot achieve a goal that requires all of your resources unless you actually have all of those resources available.

11. We cannot enter into alliances until we are acquainted with the designs of our neighbors.

12. We are not fit to lead an army on the march unless we are familiar with the face of the country – its mountains and forest, its pitfalls and precipices, its marshes and swamps.

13. We shall be unable to turn natural advantage to account unless we make use of local guides.

11. You cannot enter into co-counsel or co-defense alliances unless you know your co-party's objectives.

12. One is not fit to lead litigation unless familiar with the court rules, jurisdiction, elements of claims, standards of review, burden of proof, and facts.

13. You will be unable to take full benefit of the natural advantages in your jurisdiction without the help of local counsel.

14. In war, practice dissimulation, and you will succeed.

15. Whether to concentrate or to divide your troops must be decided in circumstances.

16. Let your rapidity be that of the wind, your compactness be that of the forest.

17. In raiding and plundering be like fire, in immovability like a mountain.

18. Let your plans be dark and impenetrable as night, and when you move, fall like a thunderbolt.

19. When you plunder countryside, let the spoil be divided amongst your men; when you capture new territory, cut it up into allotments for the benefit of the soldiery.

14. In litigation, practice the art of deception and you will succeed.

Deception does not mean breaking ethical rules. As stated earlier, deception in this book is about subtlety and misdirection. This could mean subtlety leading your opponent to believe certain evidence is important in order to distract him from pursuing other evidence more helpful to his case.

15. Whether to concentrate or divide your resources must be decided based on the circumstances then before you.

16. When you intend to act quickly, act very quickly, like the wind. When you intend to consolidate your energy or resources, compact your energy or resources like the forest.

17. When striking quickly, be powerful and overwhelming like fire. When taking a static position, be immoveable like a mountain.

18. Keep your strategy and tactics secret, but when you move, strike like a thunderbolt.

19. Share your winnings with your staff. Give those that seek it more responsibility as you grow the firm.

20. Ponder and deliberate before you make a move.

21. He will conquer who has learnt the artifice of deviation. Such is the art of maneuvering.

22. The Book of Army Managements says: On the field of battle, the spoken word does not carry far enough: Hence the institution of gongs and drums. Nor can ordinary objects be seen clearly enough: Hence the institution of banners and flags.   Gongs and drums, banners and flags, are means whereby the ears and eyes of the host may be focused on one particular point.

23. The host thus forming a single united body, it is impossible either for the brave to advance alone, or for the cowardly to retreat alone. This is the art of handling larges masses of men.

24. In night-fighting, then, make much use of signal-fires and drums, and in fighting by day, or flags and banners, as a means of influencing the ears and eyes of your army.

20. Ponder and deliberate your moves before you make them.

21. The litigator who thinks creatively or "outside the box" will win battles. This is the art of maneuvering.

22. Use technology to maintain communication with your team and co-counsel. When properly used, the team will know their roles, be easily managed, and remain confident in the cause.

23. By keeping your team well-informed, you will be able to ensure that the brave do not advance alone, or the fearful retreat alone. This is the art of communication amongst big teams.

24. Employ the appropriate method of communication, which may be email or fax while at the office and texts, emails, or calls at night.

25. A whole army may be robbed of its spirit; a commander-in-chief may be robbed of his presence of mind.

26. Now a soldier's spirit is keenest in the morning; by noonday it has begun to flag; and in the evening, his mind is bent only on returning to camp.

27. A clever general, therefore, avoids an army when its spirit is keen, but attacks it when it is sluggish and inclined to return. This is the art of studying moods.

28. Disciplined and calm, to await the appearance of disorder and hubbub amongst the enemy: This is the art of retaining self-possession.

29. To be near the goal while the enemy is still far from it, to wait at ease while the enemy is toiling and struggling to be well fed while the enemy is famished: - This is the art of husbanding one's strength.

25. It is possible to rob a team of its spirit. It is also possible to cause an attorney to lose his calm or control of the matter.

26. A person is most astute in the morning. By lunchtime, his senses have begun to dull. By the evening, his mind is only on returning home.

27. With this in mind, a clever attorney will avoid his opponent when he is most aware, and attack when his opponent is sluggish and thinking about returning home. This is the art of studying moods.

In litigation, you may want to take the deposition of the opposing party in the afternoon on a Friday, while having your witness deposed on a Monday morning. Judges right before lunch will be less astute, but early in the morning or after they have eaten may produce more carefully thought out actions.

28. Remain calm and wait for your opponent to become agitated. This is the art of retaining self-control.

29. Be well prepared and calm before the battle, while your opponent is tired and toiling away for more time or information. This is the art of conserving your strength.

30. To refrain from intercepting an enemy whose banners are in perfect order, to refrain from attacking an army drawn up in calm and confident array: - This is the art of studying circumstances.

31. It is a military axiom not to advance uphill against the enemy, nor to oppose him when he comes downhill.

32. Do not pursue an enemy who simulates flight; do not attack soldiers whose temper is keen.

33. Do no swallow bait offered by the enemy.

34. Do not interfere with an army that is returning home.

35. When you surround an army, leave an outlet free. Do not press a desperate foe too hard.

36. Such is the art of warfare.

30. Be careful about attacking a well-organized opponent who is calm and confident. This is the art of studying circumstances.

31. It is a military truth that you do not advance uphill against the enemy or oppose him while his is coming downhill. Avoid those issues where momentum and strength are on the side of your opponent.

32. Do not pursue a position that your opponent appears to be offering as an area of weakness, or pursue an issue where your opponent is enthusiastic to engage you.

33. Do not swallow bait offered by your opponent.

34. Do not agitate an opponent who is wrapping up his affairs and settling the matter. Do not give him a reason to change his mind.

35. When you engage your opponent, leave a path to settlement open. Do not press a desperate opponent too hard, as this causes fiercer fighting rather than giving up.

36. This is the art of warfare.

8
VARIATION IN TACTICS

Sun Tzu said:

1. In war, the general receives his commands from the sovereign, collects his army and concentrates his forces.

2. When in difficult country, do not encamp. In country where high roads intersect, join hands with your allies. Do not linger in dangerously isolated positions. In hemmed-in situations, you must resort to stratagem. In desperate positions, you must fight.

3. There are roads which must not be followed. Armies which must not be attacked. Towns which must not be besieged, positions which must not be contested. Commands of the sovereign which must not be obeyed.

4. The general who thoroughly understands the advantages that accompany variation of tactics knows who to handle his troops.

5. The general, who does not understand these, may be well acquainted with the configuration of the country, yet he will not be able to turn his knowledge to practical account.

1. In litigation, after the attorney receives his directive from the client, he gathers his staff and concentrates his resources.

2. When knee-deep in a difficult issue, do not rest.

In litigation where your goals are in tandem with a co-party, join forces. Do not keep the focus on bad positions or issues that you face. When you are surrounded by bad facts, you must resort to strategy. When in a desperate situation, you must fight.

3. There are arguments which should not be raised. There are opponents which should not be attacked. There are matters which should not be brought, and positions that should not be contested. There are also commands of the client which should not be obeyed.

4. The attorney that understands the advantages that flow from the variation of tactics also knows how to handle his staff.

5. The attorney who does not understand the nature of varying tactics may still be a brilliant attorney, yet his failure to understand people will prevent him from turning his knowledge into practical application.

6. So, the student of war who is unversed in the art of war of varying his plans, even though he is acquainted with the Five Advantages, will fail to make the best use of his men.

7. Hence in the wise leader's plans, considerations of advantage and of disadvantage will be blended together.

8. If our expectation of advantage be tempered in this way, we may succeed in accomplishing the essential part of our schemes.

9. If, on the other hand, in the midst of difficulties we are always ready to seize an advantage, we may extricate ourselves from misfortune.

10. Reduce the hostile chiefs by inflicting damage on them; and make trouble for them, and keep them constantly engaged; hold out specious allurements, and make them rush to any given point.

11. The art of war teaches us to rely not on the likelihood of the enemy's not coming, but on our own readiness to receive him; not on the chance of his not attacking, but rather on the fact that we have made our position unassailable.

6. However, be cautious. The student of litigation who knows the justness of the cause, the court, the facts, the commanders, and the methods and discipline, will still fail to make the best of his case if he does not know how to vary his plans.

7. The wise leader's plans blend together the advantages and disadvantages that are present in the matter.

8. If you are able to consider how your well-laid plans could fail, then you can succeed in accomplishing at least the essential parts of your objective.

9. Further, if you are able to maintain a positive attitude when times get tough, then you can avoid misfortune.

10. Reduce the effectiveness of hostile opposing counsel by inflicting damage on his positions, making trouble for him and keeping him constantly engaged. Hold out false profits to make him rush to argue any given point.

11. The art of war teaches you not to rely on the possibility that litigation will occur, but rather to plan for when it does.

Further, it is not about whether a position will be attacked, but rather what you have done to make that position unassailable.

12. There are five dangerous faults which may affect a general:

     (1)   Recklessness, which leads to destruction;

     (2)   Cowardice, which lead to capture;

     (3)   A hasty temper, which can be provoked by insults;

     (4)   A delicacy of honor which is sensitive to shame;

     (5)   Over-solicitude for his men, which exposes him to worry and trouble.

13. These are the five besetting sins of a general, ruinous to the conduct of war.

14. When an army is overthrown and its leader slain, the cause will surely be found amongst these five dangerous faults. Let them be a subject of meditation.

12. There are five dangerous personality traits which may affect a leader:

1) Recklessness, which leads to destruction;

2) Cowardice, which leads to capture;

3) Quick to anger, which can be provoked by insults;

4) Reputation-focused, which is sensitive to shame; and

5) Overly sensitive, which exposes him to worry and concern.

13. These are the five negative personality traits of a leader which are ruinous to the conduct of the matter.

14. When a major loss occurs that causes the failure of even the attorneys working on the matter, the underlying cause will undoubtedly be due to one of these.

These five negative personality traits should be the subject of reflection and meditation.

9
THE ARMY ON THE MARCH

Sun Tzu said:

1. We come now to the question of encamping the army, and observing signs of the enemy. Pass quickly over mountains, and keep in the neighborhood of valleys.

2. Camp in high places, facing the sun. Do not climb heights in order to fight. So much for mountain warfare.

3. After crossing a river, you should get far away from it.

4. When an invading force crosses a river in its onward march, do not advance to meet in mid-stream. It will be best to let half the army get across, and then deliver your attack.

5. If you are anxious to fight, you should not go to meet the invader near a river which has to cross.

6. Moor your craft higher up than the enemy, and facing the sun. Do not move up-stream to meet the enemy. So much for river warfare.

1. We now come to the topic of choosing themes for the case, and of observing our opponent. Pass quickly over themes which are lofty, instead sticking to those that can be easily followed.

2. Rest on themes which are welcoming in the light of day. Focus on those that are grounded and do not require lofty thoughts to understand.

3. After addressing a negative aspect of your case, you should move far away from it.

4. When your opponent is addressing a negative aspect of his case, do not pounce on the issue when he first begins to discuss it. Instead, let some of his argument develop before you intervene with your attack

5. If you are anxious to deliver your argument, stay away from your opponent until he has begun addressing the negative aspects of his case.

6. Develop a theme for your case, and stick with that theme as you shine a spotlight on it. Do not maneuver your position to meet your opponent. Your position is correct and your opponent needs to meet you, versus you moving to meet him.

7. In crossing sale-marshes, your sole concern should be to get over them quickly, without any delay.

8. If forced to fight in a salt-marsh, you should have water and grass near you, and get your back to a clump of trees. So much for operations in salt-marshes.

9. In dry, level country, take up an easily accessible position with rising ground to your right and on your rear, so that the danger may be in front and safety lie behind. So much for campaigning in flat country.

10. These are the four useful branches of military knowledge which enabled the Yellow Emperor to vanquish four other sovereigns.

11. All armies prefer high ground to low, and sunny places to dark.

12. If you are careful of your men and camp on hard ground, the army will be free from disease of every kind, and this will spell victory.

7. In addressing issues that bog your case down like a marsh, your sole concern should be to clear confusion as quickly as possible.

8. If you are forced to fight on an issue which is difficult to understand or overly complicates a matter, then you should have well developed evidence or resources, and some kind of key assistance (for example, an expert witness) supporting your position.

9. In cases where the issues are straightforward and easy to understand, develop your evidence to provide support for each of your elements, and have a simple theme to lead your case.

Support each of your elements so that your focus is on presenting your theme; your evidence offers the foundation to fight from.

10. These are four useful pieces of information which help the litigation attorney win trials.

11. All litigators prefer to have the better theme that shines under the spotlight, versus bad themes that do not stand up to scrutiny.

12. If you take care of your staff and adopt solid themes, your team will be free from stress and illness, which will aid you in obtaining victory.

13. When you come to a hill or a bank, occupy the sunny side, with the slope on your right rear. Thus you will at once act for the benefit of your soldiers and utilize the natural advantages of the ground.

14. When, in consequence of heavy rains up-country, a river which you wish to ford is swollen and flecked with foam, you must wait until it subsides.

15. Country in which there are precipitous cliffs with torrents running between, deep natural hollows, confined places, tangled thickets quagmires and crevasses, should be left with all possible speed and not approached.

16. While we keep away from such places, we should get the enemy to approach them; while we face them, we should let the enemy have them on his rear.

17. In the neighborhood of your camp there should not be any hilly country, ponds surrounded by aquatic grass, hollow basins filled with reeds, or woods with thick undergrowth, they must be carefully routed out and searched; for these are places where men in ambush or insidious spies are likely to be lurking.

18. When the enemy is close at hand and remains quiet, he is relying on the natural strength of his position.

13. When you meet resistance on an issue, take the high ground in arguing the matter. This reflects well on you and your team, and utilizes the natural advantages of being the bigger person.

14. When an already negative situation is further aggravated, preventing you from effectively addressing it, wait until the issue has subsided before you act.

15. Matters where there are terrible facts with terrible law running in between, with hidden issues, unknown surprises, bad witnesses, and tough clients, are matters that should be avoided as much as possible.

16. While you should avoid bad cases like this, you should work to get your opponent to view his position this way. You should be facing your opponent's disastrous case, while he is stuck in it.

17. As you develop your case, there should not be any evidentiary or factual issues which are unclear or obfuscated to you. You should carefully research all the facts so you are not surprised.

18. When your opponent confronts you and is calm, he is relying on the natural strength of his position.

19. When he keeps aloof and tries to provoke a battle, he is anxious for the other side to advance.

20. If his placed of encampment is easy to access, he is tendering bait.

21. Movement amongst the trees of a forest shows that the enemy is advancing. The appearance of a number of screens in the midst of thick grass means that the enemy wants to make us suspicious.

22. The rising of birds in their flight is the sign of an ambush. Startled beasts indicate that a sudden attack is coming.

23. When there is dust rising in a high column, it is the sign of chariots advancing; when the dust is low, bus spread over a wide area; it betokens the approach of infantry. When it branches out in different directions, it shows that parties have been sent to collect firewood. A few clouds of dust moving to and fro signify that the army is encamping.

19. When your opponent is unfriendly and distant, and tries to provoke a battle, he is anxious for you to act.

20. If your opponent's position appears too easy to attack, then it is a trap.

21. Consolidation of witnesses, facts, or issues means your opponent is advancing. The presentment of a number of issues without clear direction means your opponent wants you to become concerned and suspicious.

22. Unusual movement or communication by your opponent or by expert witnesses, witnesses, or other third parties indicates an attack is coming.

23. After a considerable amount of movement from opposing counsel, a dispositive motion is coming. When there is a small amount of movement or communication, a non-dispositive motion or request for a hearing is coming. When this movement is scattered, it means evidence is being gathered. When there is sporadic movement, it means no attack is imminent.

This paragraph tells us that you can anticipate your opponent's next move through his preparatory actions.

24. Humble words and increased preparations are signs that the enemy is about to advance. Violent language and driving forward as if to the attack are signs that he will retreat.

25. When the light chariots come out first and take up a position on the wings, it is a sign that the enemy is forming for battle.

26. Peace proposals unaccompanied by a sworn covenant indicate a plot.

27. When there is much running about and the soldiers fall into rank, it means that the critical moment has come.

28. When some are seen advancing and some retreating, it is a lure.

29. When the soldiers stand leaning on their spears, they are faint from want of food.

30. If those who are sent to draw water begin by drinking themselves, the army is suffering from thirst.

31. If the enemy sees an advantage to be gained and makes no efforts to secure it, the soldiers are exhausted.

24. Humble words and increased preparations are signs that your opponent is about to attack. Whereas, unprofessional threats of an impending attack are signs that he will retreat.

25. When the preliminary, pre-dispositive issues are fully addressed, he is preparing for battle.

26. Proposals that are not definite or in writing must be treated carefully, as they may not materialize, or they may be part of a broader strategy.

27. When there is a lot of activity, and then stillness, it means the critical moment has come.

28. When your opponent is advancing positions while simultaneously withdrawing those positions, it is a lure.

29. The attorney displaying tiredness of the conflict is facing financial issues with their client or the matter.

30. Those attorneys who are sent to settle a matter but begin by maximizing their billable time, or killing the settlement discussions, are suffering from a lack of business.

31. When an opportunity to gain arises in the case but your opponent does not take it, then their client is tired of the matter.

32. If birds gather on any spot, it is unoccupied. Clamor by night betokens nervousness.

33. If there is disturbance in the camp, the general's authority is weak. If the banners and flags are shifted about, sedition is afoot. If the officers are angry, it means that the men are weary.

34. When an army feeds its horses with grain and kills its cattle for food, and when the men do not hang their cooking-pots over the camp-fires, showing that they will not return to their tents, you may know that they are determined to fight to the death.

35. The sight of men whispering together in small knots or speaking in subdued tones points to disaffection amongst the rank and file.

36. Too frequent rewards signify that the enemy is at the end of his resources; too many punishments betray a condition of dire distress.

37. To begin by bluster, but afterwards to take fright at the enemy's numbers, shows a supreme lack of intelligence.

32. Public complaints will gather about bad business practices that have not yet been the subject of litigation. An opponent secretly covering up information is a sign of nervousness.

33. If a party, or staff associate, "goes rouge," then the lead attorney's authority is weak. If each member of their team delivers a different message, then internal conflict is occurring. If the lead attorney is angry, then it means his staff is tired.

34. When an opponent spends all of his money, takes on credit, or sells possessions so that he may continue the litigation, then he is determined to fight until ruin.

35. When members of a team are seen whispering in secret away from others, then that points to dissatisfaction among the staff.

36. Giving out too frequent of rewards to keep order in the ranks signifies an end to his resources. Too much discipline or punishment indicates dire distress.

37. An attorney who begins a case with loud and aggressive talk, but later is afraid of the opponent, demonstrates a supreme lack of intelligence.

38. When envoys are sent with compliments in their mouths, it is a sign that the enemy wishes for a truce.

39. If the enemy's troops march up angrily and remain facing ours for a long time without either joining battle or taking themselves off again, the situation is one that demands great vigilance and circumspection.

40. If our troops are no more in number than the enemy that is amply sufficient; it only means that no direct attack can be made. What we can do is simply to concentrate all our available strength, keep a close watch on the enemy, and obtain reinforcements.

41. He who exercises no forethought but makes light of his opponents is sure to be captured by them.

42. If soldiers are punished before they have grown attached to you, they will not prove submissive; and, unless submissive, they will be practically useless. If, when the soldiers have become attached to you, punishments are not enforced, they will still be useless.

43. Therefore, soldiers must be treated in the first instance with humanity, but kept under control by means of iron discipline. This is a certain road to victory.

38. When an opponent comes to you with compliments about how well you are handling the matter, then it is a sign that he would like to settle.

39. If your opponent comes to you angrily or in a threatening tone about some aspect of the matter, but does not take action for a long time, then the situation demands great care. You should be vigilant that he may be developing an attack outside your view.

40. If the strength of your case is as strong as the strength of your opponents, then you should not directly attack. Instead, you should concentrate your arguments, keep a close watch on where your opponent is headed, and obtain reinforcements (perhaps more discovery, experts, or witness testimony).

41. One who does not plan ahead while mocking his opponents is sure to lose to them.

42. If you discipline staff before they have grown attached to you, then they will not follow your direction, and be practically useless. Once they become attached to you, you must enforce discipline or then they too will become useless.

43. Therefore, you should treat your staff with compassion and fellowship. However, you must enforce discipline, as this is the certain road to victory.

44. If in training soldiers commands are habitually enforced, the army will be well-disciplined; if not, its discipline will be bad.

45. If a general shows confidence in his men but always insists on his orders being obeyed, the gain will be mutual.

44. If you apply discipline consistently among your staff, then they will be well-disciplined. If you do not apply it consistently, then they will not be.

45. If you show faith in your staff's ability, but still insist on your orders being obeyed, then your gain and your staff's gain will be mutual.

10
TERRAIN

Sun Tzu said:

1. We may distinguish six kinds of terrain, to wit: 1) accessible ground; 2) entangling ground; 3) temporizing ground; 4) narrow passes; 5) precipitous heights; 6) positions at a great distance from the enemy.

2. Ground which can be freely traversed by both sides is called accessible. With regard to ground of this nature, be before the enemy in occupying the raised and sunny spots, and carefully guard your line of supplies. Then you will be able to fight with advantage.

3. Ground which can be abandoned but is hard to reoccupy is called entangling. Form a position of this sort, if the enemy is unprepared, you may sally forth and defeat him. But if the enemy is prepared for your coming, and you fail to defeat him, then, return being impossible, disaster will ensue.

4. When the position is such that neither side will gain by making the first move, it is called temporizing ground. In a position of this sort, even though the enemy should offer us attractive bait, it will be advisable not to stir forth, but rather to retreat, thus enticing the enemy in his turn; then, when part of his army has come out, we may deliver our attack with advantage.

1. We may classify evidence into six categories 1) Equal, 2) Entangling, 3) Delayed, 4) Negative, 5) Positive, and 6) Gaping.

2. Evidence available to both sides to claim as helpful for their cause can be defined as Equal. In selecting this kind of evidence, choose the positive evidence that helps you appear as if you are taking the "higher road."

3. Evidence that is hard to reclaim as helpful to your case once you have abandoned it is called Entangling evidence. For this kind of evidence, if you attempt to reclaim it and your opponent is not prepared, then you can still use it to your advantage. However, if you attempt to reclaim the evidence and your opponent is prepared, then you will lose the issue if you fail in your efforts.

4. Evidence that is negative for whichever side brings it up first is called Delayed evidence. With this kind of evidence, you should not succumb to attractive offers from opposing counsel to first present the evidence. Instead, you should remain submissive so that your opponent must act first, at which time you can pounce with the advantage.

5. With regard to narrow passes, if you can occupy them first, let them be strongly garrisoned and wait the advent of the enemy. Should the army forestall you in occupying a pass, do not go after him if the pass is fully garrisoned, but only if it is weakly garrisoned.

6. With regard to precipitous heights, if you are beforehand with your adversary, you should occupy the raised and sunny spots, and there wait for him to come up. If the enemy has occupied them before you, do not follow him, but retreat and try to entice him away.

7. If you are situated at a great distance from the enemy, and the strength of the two armies is equal, it is not easy to provoke a battle, and fighting will be to your disadvantage.

8. These six are the principles connected with Earth. The general who has attained a responsible post must be careful to study them.

5. Negative evidence is damaging evidence that is more beneficial for you to disclose first. If you can completely address the negative evidence, then you can diffuse any issues it presents. However, should your opponent deliver the negative information ahead of you, then you should not address it in detail if your opponent's presentation was thorough. If his presentation was not thorough, then you may fully address it yourself.

6. Positive evidence is good and productive evidence that forces your opponent to follow your arguments in order to make his own. If your opponent has control of the positive arguments, do not follow him, but step back and try to entice him into a position more favorable to you.

7. Gaping evidence is that which is viewed completely differently by each side, based on the point of view taken. If the argument flowing from the Gaping evidence is equally persuasive for each side, then you should not attempt to first address why their perspective is wrong. The advantage is in presenting your perspective first, and having your opponent follow your position with his arguments.

8. These are the six kinds of evidence connected with the Facts of the Case (factor three). The attorney who has obtained a place of responsibility must carefully study them.

9. Now an army is exposed to six several calamities, not arising from natural causes, but from faults for which the general is responsible. These are: 1)Flight; 2) insubordination; 3) collapse; 4)ruin; 5) disorganization; and 6)rout.

10. Other conditions being equal, if one force is hurled against another ten times its size, the result will be flight of the former.

11. When the common soldiers are too strong and their officers too weak, the result is insubordination.

12. When the officers are too strong and the common soldiers too weak, the results collapse.

13. When the higher officers are angry and insubordinate, and on meeting the enemy gives battle on their own account from a feeling of resentment, before the commander-in-chief can tell whether or not he is a position to fight, the result is ruin.

14. When the general is weak and without authority; when his orders are not clear and distinct; when there are no fixed duties assigned to officers and men and the ranks are formed in a slovenly haphazard manner, the result is utter disorganization.

9. A legal team can be exposed to six different calamities that arise from poor management, rather than from nature. They are: 1) Flight, 2) Insubordination, 3) Collapse, 4) Ruin, 5) Disorganization, and 6) Retreat

10. Other things being equal, if one legal team is forced to fight another that is ten times it size, then the result will be the flight of the smaller.

11. When the associates on the case are smarter than the lawyer in command, the result will be insubordination.

12. When the lawyer in command is not supported by associates that are as capable as he, then the results will be collapse.

13. When an associate who is charged with leading specific matters is angry and insubordinate, and engages the opponent due to a feeling of resentment, and then acts before the commanding attorney can tell whether he is in a position to fight, the result is ruin.

14. When the lead attorney is weak and without authority, when his orders are not clear or distinct, when there are no fixed duties assigned to the team, and when the ranks are haphazardly managed, then the result is utter disorganization.

15. When a general, unable to establish the enemy's strength, allows an inferior force to engage a larger one, or hurls a weak detachment against a powerful one, and neglects to place picked soldiers in the front rank, the result must be rout.

16. These are six ways of courting defeat, which must be carefully noted by the general who has attained a responsible post.

17. The natural information of the country is the soldier's best ally; but a power of estimating the adversary, of controlling the forces of victory, and of shrewdly calculating difficulties, dangers and distances, constitutes the test of a great general.

18. He who knows these things, and in fighting puts his knowledge into practice, will win his battles. He who knows them not, nor practices them, will surely be defeated.

15. When the lead attorney is unable to gauge his opponents strength and allows an inexperienced associate engage against a much more experienced one, or takes an inferior position against a much better one, then the result will be retreat.

16. These six previous calamities that arise from poor management are six ways of courting defeat. They should be carefully noted by the attorney who has obtained a post of responsibility.

17. You may be able to win a case simply because you are in your home jurisdiction, but the test of a great attorney is found in estimating his opponent, controlling the forces of victory, plus shrewdly calculating the difficulties he will face, the dangers present for his client, and the resources required to win.

18. If you know these things, and put this knowledge into practice, then you will win cases. If you do not know these things, or do not know how to employ them, then you will surely be defeated.

19. If fighting is sure to result in victory, then you must fight, even though the ruler forbid it; if fighting will not result in victory, then you not fight even at the ruler's bidding.

20. The general who advances without coveting fame and retreats without fearing disgrace, whose only thought is to protect his country and do good service for his sovereign, is the jewel of the kingdom.

21. Regard your solders as your children, and they will follow you into the deepest valleys; look upon them as your own beloved sons, and they will stand by you even unto death.

19. If you are assured of victory taking an action that your client has discouraged, then you should take it despite the conflicting direction. If you are assured of defeat by taking some other action that your client has demanded, then you should not take it despite that conflicting direction.

The first sentence of this paragraph could be a little challenging for attorneys who cannot act outside their client's express directives, but the message here is conveyed as by Sun Tzu. The second sentence should pose less of an issue for attorneys, because it may be appropriate for an attorney to refrain from taking an action demanded by the client for a number of reasons.

Finally, you should take care not to overestimate your own ability, or follow the advice of this paragraph unless capable and unless you understand the nuances of this book.

20. The attorney who engages in litigation without coveting fame or viewing a loss as a disgrace, and who is only concerned about meeting his clients' objectives, is a jewel of the profession.

21. Regard your staff as your children and they will follow you through the hardest challenges. Look upon them as your beloved sons and daughters and they will stand by you until the end.

22. If, however, you are indulgent, but unable to make your authority felt; kind-hearted, but unable to enforce your commands; and incapable, moreover, of quelling disorder: Then your soldiers must be likened to spoilt children; they are useless for any practical purpose.

24. If we know that our own men are in a condition to attack, but are unaware that the enemy is not open to attack, we have gone halfway towards victory.

25. If we know that the enemy is open to attack, but are unaware that our own men are not in a condition to attack, we have gone only half way towards victory.

26. If we know that the enemy is open to attack, and also knowing our men are in a condition to attack, but are unaware that the nature of the ground makes fighting impracticable, we have still gone only halfway towards victory.

27. Hence the experienced soldier, once in motion, is never bewildered; once he has broken camp, he is never at a loss.

28. Hence the saying: If you know the enemy and know yourself, your victory will not stand in doubt; if you know Heaven and know Earth, you may make your victory complete.

23. However, if you are overly lenient and unable to establish your authority, or too kind and unable to enforce discipline, or incapable of controlling disorder, then your staff will be like spoiled children and be useless for any practical purpose.

24. If you know your team is ready to attack, but unaware that your opponent cannot be defeated, then you are only halfway to victory.

25. If you know your opponent can be successfully attacked, but unaware that your team is not yet ready, then you are only halfway to victory.

26. If you know your team is ready to attack and that your opponent can be defeated, but unaware that the jurisdiction makes fighting impractical, then you still are only halfway to victory.

27. Hence, once the experienced litigator begins to execute his strategy, he is never caught off guard by events that unfold.

28. If you know the enemy and know yourself, then your victory will never be in doubt. If you know the Court and the facts also, then your victory is assured.

11
THE NINE SITUATIONS

Sun Tzu said:

1. The art of war recognizes nine varieties of ground: 1) Dispersive ground; 2) facile ground; 3) contentious ground; 4) open ground; 5) ground of intersecting highways; 6) serious ground; 7) difficult ground; 8) hemmed-in ground; and 9)desperate ground.

2. When a chieftain is fighting in his own territory, it is dispersive ground.

3. When he has penetrated into hostile territory, but to no great distance, if it facile ground.

4. Ground the possession of which imports great advantage to either side, is contentious ground.

5. Ground on which each side has liberty of movement is open ground.

6. Ground which forms the key to three contiguous states, so that he who occupies it first has most of the Empire at his command, is a ground of intersection highways.

7. When an army has penetrated into the heart of a hostile country, leaving a number of fortified cities in its rear, it is serious ground.

1. The art of war recognizes nine variations of ground, equating to the following kinds of jurisdictions: 1) Friendly, 2) Effortless, 3) Contentious, 4) Open, 5) Focal, 6) Serious, 7) Difficult, 8) Biased, and 9) Desperate.

2. When an attorney is fighting within his own jurisdiction, it is Friendly.

3. When an attorney is slightly outside his own jurisdiction, but is within in his opponent's, then it is Effortless.

4. When the jurisdiction could provide great advantage to either side, it is Contentious.

5. A court that enables both parties free movement to establish their respective case, then it is Open.

6. When the litigation involves multiple parties that converge in litigation in one jurisdiction, so that alliances can be established with co-parties, then it is Focal.

7. When one must litigate far away from home and in the heart of the opponent's jurisdiction, then the jurisdiction is Serious.

8. Mountain forests rugged steeps, marshes and fens – all country that is hard to traverse: This is difficult ground.

9. Ground which is reached through narrow gorges and from which we can only retire by tortuous paths, so that a small number of the enemy would suffice to crush a large body of our men this is hemmed-in ground.

10. Ground, on which we can only be saved from destruction by fighting without delay, is desperate ground.

11. On dispersive ground, therefore, fight not. On facile ground, halt not. On contentious ground, attack not.

12. On open ground, do not try to block the enemy's way.

13. On the ground of intersection highways, join hands with your allies.

14. On serious ground, gather in plunder. In difficult ground, keep steadily in the march.

15. On hemmed-in ground, resort to stratagem. On desperate ground, fight.

8. A Difficult jurisdiction is one that has multiple layers of complex rules, procedures, and customs that are hard for an inexperienced outsider to know.

9. A jurisdiction that is so prejudiced and unfriendly that it will take very little effort for your opponent to crush your position is a jurisdiction that is Biased.

10. A fight within a jurisdiction that must be conducted with the utmost speed in order to avoid loss is one that is Desperate.

11. In a Friendly jurisdiction, do not raise the court's anger. In an Effortless jurisdiction, proceed by leading the court on the path you have laid. In a Contentious jurisdiction, do not display overly aggressive behavior.

12. In an Open jurisdiction, block your opponent's ability to move or collect information.

13. In a Focal jurisdiction, join forces with your co-parties.

14. In a Serious jurisdiction, utilize local counsel and local resources. In a Difficult jurisdiction, constantly review the local rules and procedures to ensure they are regularly followed.

15. In a Biased jurisdiction, use strategy. In a Desperate jurisdiction, fight without delay.

16. Those who were called skilful leaders of old knew how to drive a wedge between the enemy's front and rear; to prevent co-operation between his large and small divisions; to hinder the good troops from rescuing the bad, the officers from rallying their men.

17. When the enemy's men were united, they managed to keep them in disorder.

18. When it was to their advantage, they made a forward move; when otherwise, they stopped still.

19. If asked how to cope with a great host of the enemy in orderly array and on the point of marching to the attack, I should say: "Begin by seizing something which your opponent holds dear; then he will be amenable to your will".

20. Rapidity is the essence of ware: take advantage of the enemy's unreadiness, make your way by unexpected routes, and attack unguarded spots.

21. The following are the principles to be observed by an invading force: The further you penetrate into a country the greater will be the solidarity of your troops, and thus the defenders will not prevail against you.

16. The old leaders skilled in warfare knew how to drive a wedge between the enemy's positions to prevent coordination of the cause, the teams, and from allowing one position to be able to save another.

17. These leaders were able to keep their opponents in disorder, even when they appeared to be united.

18. When advantageous, they pressed their position. Then they stopped advancing when no longer helpful.

19. If you are facing an organized opponent that is at the point of attacking your position, seize or seek out something that he holds dear and he will bend to your will.

20. Speed is the essence of war – to take advantage of your opponent not being ready, taking routes and positions that are unexpected, and to attack positions that are not guarded.

21. One can observe that the further into a hostile jurisdiction that your team travels, the more they will function as a team and rely upon one another. This will prevent your opponent from prevailing against you (all other things being equal).

22. Make forays in fertile country in order to supply your army with food.

23. Carefully study the well-being of your men, and do not overtax them. Concentrate your energy and hoard your strength. Keep your army continually on the move, and devise unfathomable plans.

24. Throw your soldiers into positions whence there is no escape, and they will prefer death to flight. If they will face death, there is nothing they may not achieve. Officers and men alike will put forth their uttermost strength.

25. Soldiers when in desperate straits lose the sense of fear. If there is no place of refuge, they will stand firm. If they are in hostile country, they will show a stubborn front. If there is no help for it, they will fight hard.

26. Thus, without to be marshaled, the soldiers will be constantly on the qui vive; without waiting to be asked, they will do your will; without restrictions, they will be faithful; without giving orders, they can be trusted.

22. Maintain profitable clients with your contingency work, so that the firm may survive.

23. Carefully study the well-being of your team and do not overwork them. Conserve their energy and strength, but keep them constantly busy. The plans you draft should be incapable of being fully understood or explored.

24. Throw your staff into a position where there will be no settlement, and they will prefer to prepare for trial than throw in the towel. When they know there is no alternative, there is nothing that your high and low ranking staff cannot achieve.

25. When deep into litigation in a hostile jurisdiction, your staff will lose the sense of fear. If there is no alternative to trial and no settlement available, then they will stand firm. When they receive no help, they will fight hard.

26. In this kind of situation, your staff will not need your prompting to be vigilant. They will do your bidding without being asked, remain loyal without oversight, and be trusted without orders.

27. Prohibit the taking of omens, and do away with superstitious doubts. Then, until death itself comes, no calamity need be feared.

28. If our soldiers are not overburdened with money, it is not because they have distaste for riches; if their lives are not unduly long, it is not because they are disinclined to longevity.

29. On the day they are ordered out to battle, your soldiers may weep, those sitting up wetting their garments, and those lying down letting the tears run down their cheeks. But let them once be brought to bay, and they will display the courage of a Chu or a Kuei.

30. The skilful tactician may be likened to the shuai-jan. Now the shuai-jan is a snake that is found in the Ch'ang Mountains. Strike at its head, and you will be attacked by its tail; strike at its tail, and you will be attacked by its head; strike at its middle, and you will be attacked by head and tail both.

31. Asked if an army can be made to imitate the shuai-jan, I should answer, "Yes". For the men of Wu and the men of Yueh are enemies; yet they are crossing a river in the same boat and are caught by a storm, they will come to each other's assistance just as the left hand helps the right.

27. Prohibit naysayers and those who use superstition to sow doubt. This will prevent worry among your team, even if the end result is a loss.

28. If your staff is not rich, it does not mean they dislike money. Similarly, if they work on matters that are repugnant, does not mean that they enjoy the work.

29. Before a major trial, your staff may suffer from severe stress and anxiety. However, once the trial begins, strength and courage will overcome them.

30. The skillful litigator may be likened to the Shaui-jan snake. This rapidly moving snake will attack with its tail if you strike its head, attack with its head if you strike its tail, and attack with both its head and tail if you strike its middle.

That is, the skillful litigator will have prepared for multiple contingencies and will be able to mount a counter-argument to any position taken by his opponent.

31. A team can be made to imitate this snake, even when half the team is in conflict with the other half. When there is an outside attack on their collective position, then they will put aside their differences and come to each other's aid.

32. Hence it is not enough to put one's trust in the tethering of horses, and the burying of chariot wheels in the ground.

33. The principle of which to manage an army is to set up one standard of courage which all must reach.

34. How to make the best of both strong and weak that is a question involving the proper use of ground.

35. Thus the skilful general conducts his army just as though he were leading a single man , willy-nilly, by the hand.

36. It is the business of a general to be quiet and thus ensure secrecy; upright and just, and thus maintain order.

37. He must be able to mystify his officers and men by false reports and appearances, and thus keep them in total ignorance.

32. Allaying fears of trial within your team requires more than removing methods of escape or settlement.

33. The principle to manage courage is to set up one standard that everyone must follow, including you.

34. Making the best of the strong and the weak requires an analysis of the jurisdiction you are in.

35. The skillful leader manages his entire staff as if he were leading a single member by the hand.

36. It is the lead counsel's job to be calm, secretive about his plans, honorable, and just. This is how order is maintained.

37. He must be able to mystify his top staff and keep them guessing about his strategy, to keep them in total ignorance.

This paragraph goes to the need to keep all plans secret from the opposing party, and also ensures the continuation of power seated within the top general. If your firm requires more robust leaders under the partner, then it may be helpful to stray from Sun Tzu's recommendation here. (One would imagine that Sun Tzu had one or more protégés that he shared his secrets with.)

38. By altering his arrangements and changing his plans, he keeps the enemy without definite knowledge by shirting his camp and taking circuitous routes, he prevents the enemy from anticipating his purpose.

39. At the critical moment, the leader of an army acts like one who has climbed up a height and then kicks away the ladder behind him. He carries his men deep into hostile territory before he shows his hand.

40. He burns his boats and breaks his cooking-pots; like a shepherd driving a flock of sheep, he drives his men this way and that, and northing knows whither he is going.

41. To muster his host and bring it into danger: - This may be termed the business of the general.

42. The different measures suited to the nine varieties of ground; the expediency of aggressive or defensive tactics; and the fundamental laws of human nature: These are things that must most certainly be studied.

43. When invading hostile territory, the general principle is that penetrating deeply bring cohesion; penetrating but short way means dispersion.

38. By regularly switching your direction and plans, you will keep your opponent without definite knowledge of your strategy. This will require him to expend energy and resources to follow you, and keep him from knowing your true plans.

39. At the critical moment, the lead attorney acts as someone who has climbed a ladder, then kicked it out from beneath him. He has carried his team deep into the case before showing his hand.

40. He burns the boats so there is no turning back, and destroys the cooking pots so his team must fight to eat. He acts like a shepherd driving a flock of sheep this way and that, without them knowing where they are headed.

41. The business of the general is to cause his opponent to assemble, and then be led into danger.

42. As an overview, a litigation attorney must carefully study the variations in jurisdiction, the aggressive and defensive tactics available to him, and the fundamental laws of human nature.

43. The general rule is that penetrating deep into your opponent's territory will bring cohesion among your team, but penetrating a short ways causes them to scatter.

44. When you leave your own country behind, and take your army across neighborhood territory, you find yourself on critical ground. When there are means of communication on all four sides, the ground is one of intersection highways.

45. When you penetrate deeply into a country, it is serious ground. When you penetrate but a little way, it is facile ground.

46. When you have the enemy's strongholds in your rear, and narrow passes in front, it is hemmed-in ground. When there is no place of refuge at all, it is desperate ground.

47. Therefore, on dispersive ground, I would inspire my men with unity of purpose. On facile ground, I would see that there is close connection between all parts of my army.

48. On contentious ground, I would hurry up my rear.

49. On open ground, I would keep a vigilant eye on my defenses. On ground of intersection highways, I would consolidate my alliances.

44. When you leave your own jurisdiction and go into a neighboring territory, you will be on critical ground. However, when you are able to muster the support of allies in the area, then you are in a jurisdiction that is Focal in nature.

45. When you penetrate deeply into your opponent's jurisdiction, it is a "Serious" jurisdiction. When you penetrate but a little way, it is an Effortless jurisdiction.

46. When you have the enemy's strongest positions behind you, but you are still facing a prejudicial court, you remain in a Biased jurisdiction. When you have no support for your position in the area, then you are in a Desperate jurisdiction.

47. Therefore, in a Friendly jurisdiction, you should inspire your team with unity of purpose. In an Effortless jurisdiction, you should foster a close connection within your staff.

48. In a jurisdiction where the first person there has the advantage (Contentious), you should bring your staff together as quickly as possible.

49. In a jurisdiction where the court allows the parties free movement (Open jurisdiction), you should keep an eye on your defenses. In a jurisdiction where it is possible to make local alliances, you should.

50. On serious ground, I would try to ensure a continuous stream of supplies. On difficult ground, I would keep pushing on along the road.

51. On hemmed-in ground, I would block any way of retreat. On desperate ground, I would proclaim to my soldiers the hopelessness of saving their lives.

52. For it is the soldier's disposition to offer an obstinate resistance when surrounded, to fight hard when he cannot help himself, and to obey promptly when he has fallen into danger.

53. We cannot enter into alliance with neighboring princes until we are acquainted with their designs. We are not fit to lead an army on the march unless we are familiar with the face of the country — its mountains and forests, its pitfalls and precipices, its marshes and swamps. We shall be unable to turn natural advantages to account unless we make use of local guides.

50. When litigating inside your opponent's jurisdiction (Serious), then you want to remain in constant contact with your own home base. In a jurisdiction has multiple layers of complex rules, procedures, and customs (Difficult), then you should constantly be pushing the litigation forward.

51. When in a jurisdiction that is so prejudiced and unfriendly that it will take very little effort for your opponent to crush your position (Biased), block your team from retreat or settlement if trial is your objective. When there is little hope of winning in a jurisdiction, you should tell your staff so they act courageously.

52. It is a fighter's disposition to stubbornly resist when surrounded, to fight when there is no other option, and to obey your direction when he has fallen into danger.

53. You cannot enter into co-defense or co-prosecution agreements unless you know your co-party's objectives and plans. A lead attorney is not fit to lead until he is familiar with the jurisdiction in which he is fighting, including all the positives, negatives, and keys to winning in that jurisdiction. You cannot turn natural advantages in your jurisdiction to you favor unless you know it or hire local counsel.

54. To be ignorant of any one of the following four or five principles does not befit a warlike prince.

55. When a warlike prince attacks a powerful state, his generalship shows itself in preventing the concentration of the enemy's forces. He overawes his opponents, and their allies are prevented from joining against him.

56. Hence he does not strive to ally himself with all and sundry, nor does he foster the power of other states. He carriers out his secret designs, keeping his antagonists in awe. Thus he is able to capture these cities and overthrow their kingdoms.

57. Bestow rewards without regard to rule, issue orders without regard to previous arrangements; and you will be able to handle a whole army as though you had to do with but a single man.

54. Pay attention to the following concepts, as being ignorant of them does not befit a team leader.

55. When you forcefully and preemptively attack a powerful opponent, you prevent the concentration of your opponent's forces. This can also intimidate your opponents' allies, who will carefully consider whether they want to join a fight against you.

56. Hence, you should not seek out every form of ally to help you, nor foster the power of other firms. By carrying out your own secret plans, you will keep your opponents wondering about you. This way, you will be able to succeed in your venture.

57. Give rewards outside of what your team expects, and also change direction without regard to previous plans.

Acting in this way creates an organization dependent on you, enabling you to move an entire organization as if it were just one person. Acting this way, staff does not independently think but rather follows your instructions simply because you give them. They do not know what your plans are or what is next, but rather know that your actions are never what they appear to be, so they should just trust in your direction.

This paragraph may not offer great assistance to a law firm that wants to develop strong independent attorneys, but may be helpful in a firm that needs a number of workers to follow one leader.

58. Confront your soldiers with the deed itself; never let them know your design. When the outlook is bright, bring it before their eyes; but tell them nothing when the situation is gloomy.

59. Place your army in deadly peril and it will survive; plunge it into desperate straits and it will come off in safety.

60. For it is precisely when a force has fallen into harm's way that is capable of striking a blow for victory.

61. Success in warfare is gained by carefully accommodating ourselves to the enemy's purpose.

62. By persistently hanging on the enemy's flank, we shall succeed in the long run in killing the commander-in-chief.

63. This is called the ability to accomplish a thing by sheer cunning.

64. One the day that you take up your command, block the frontier passes, destroy the official tallies, and stop the passage of all emissaries.

58. If you use this management style, do not share your plans with your team, only direct them to act once you decide to.

When the outlook is bright, share that fact with them. However, when problems are on the horizon, do not tell them.

59. Place your team in dire straits and it will survive. Plunge your team into a desperate situation, and they will come out safely.

60. It is precisely when your team is faced with huge obstacles that it becomes the most capable of dealing with them, providing you the best opportunity to win.

61. Being successful in litigation absolutely requires carefully reviewing your opponent's position, plans, and designs.

62. By persistently attacking a position that is weak, you can succeed in winning the entire case.

63. This is called the ability to accomplish something by sheer cunning.

64. On the day that you take over a matter, take steps to eliminate outside influences of your command.

65. Be stern in the council-chamber, so that you may control the situation.

66. If the enemy leaves a door open, you must rush in.

67. Forestall your opponent by seizing what he hold dear, and subtly contrive to time his arrival on the ground.

68. Walk in the path defined by rule, and accommodate yourself to the enemy until you can fight a decisive battle.

69. At first, then, exhibit the coyness of a maiden, until the enemy gives you an opening; afterwards emulate the rapidity of a running hare, and it will be too late for the enemy to oppose you.

65. Be stern with other co-counsel who may seek to exert control over your case, so that you can control your strategy and the matter.

66. If you opponent leaves a door open, then you should rush in.

67. Hinder your opponent by seizing what he holds dear, and try to time when he will take actions in the case.

68. Follow the rules laid out here, and wait to attack your opponent until you can fight and win.

69. First, display coyness to your opponent until he gives you an opening. After that, emulate the rapidness of a rabbit so that it will be too late for him to oppose you.

12
ATTACK BY FIRE

Sun Tzu said:

1. There are five ways to attacking with fire. The first is to burn soldiers in their camp; the second is to burn stores; the third is to burn baggage trains; the forth is to burn arsenals and magazines; the fifth is to hurl dropping fire amongst the enemy.

2. In order to carry out an attack, we must have means available. The material for raising fire should always be kept in readiness.

3. There is a proper season for making attacks with fire, and special days for starting a conflagration.

4. The proper season is when the weather is very dry; the special days are those when the moon is in the constellations of the Sieve, the Wall, the Wing or the Cross-bar; for these four are all days of rising wind.

1. There are five types of scorched earth tactics, which are where you make arguments that burn bridges with your opponent. They are to: 1) engage in personal attacks against the opposing party; 2) attack gains that your opponent unjustly acquired; 3) make public attacks to develop negative publicity; 4) attack opposing counsel personally; and 5) attack the opponent's claims or defenses.

2. In order to carry out such an attack, you must have the facts available to do so. You should have plans for this kind of attack ready, if needed.

3. There is a proper kind of case for making such an attack, and special moments for employing them.

4. The proper kind of case is where the litigation environment is acrimonious. The special moments are those when the use of inflammatory language will sway the decision maker.

5. In attacking with fire, one should be prepared to meet five possible developments:

(1) When fire breaks out inside the enemy's camp, respond at once with an attack from without.

(2) If there is an outbreak of fire, but the enemy's soldiers remain quiet, bide your time and do not attack.

(3) When the force of the flames has reached its height, follow it up with an attack, if that is practicable; if not, stay where you are.

(4) If it is possible to make an assault with fire from without, do not wait for it to break out within, but deliver your attack at a favorable moment.

(5) When you start a fire, be to windward of it. Do not attack from the leeward.

6. A wind that rises in the daytime lasts long, but a night breeze soon falls.

5. In attacking with scorched earth tactics, you should be prepare for five possible developments:

(1) When your tactics result in your opponent's focus being shifted towards defending the tactics, then you can immediately follow up with an attack on the issues.

(2) If your tactics do not sway your opponent to act, then do not press further at this time.

(3) If your use of scorched earth tactics results in the court being swayed by their use, then follow up immediately by tying the attack to the issues.

(4) If you can make a scorched earth point without directly doing so, then hold your direct attack for when an opportunity presents itself.

(5) When you employ these kinds of tactics, be careful that they do not come back to burn you. Be careful about attacking people or positions valued by the decision maker.

6. Making bold and direct scorched earth attacks under the right conditions will have long-term lingering effects. Making minor or half-hearted attacks will not.

7. In every army, the five developments connected with fire must be known, the movements of the stars calculated, and a watch kept for the proper days.

8. Hence those who use fire as an aid to the attack show intelligence; those who use water as an aid to the attack gain an accession of strength.

9. By means of water, an enemy may be intercepted, but not robbed of all his belongings.

10. Unhappy is the fate of one who tries to win his battles and succeed in his attacks without cultivating the spirit of enterprise; for the result is waste of time and general stagnation.

11. Hence the saying: The enlightened ruler lays his plans well ahead; the good general cultivates his resources.

12. No ruler should put troops into the field merely to gratify his own spleen; no general should fight a battle simply out of pique.

13. If it is to your advantage, make a forward move; it not, stays where you are.

7. In each matter, the use of scorched earth tactics must be known and planned for (offensively and defensively), and the conditions for their use known, so they can be properly deployed.

8. Those that know how to employ these tactics show intelligence. Those who shrewdly use a repentant or humble attitude to aid in the attack, add to the strength of it.

9. Using humility will assist you in making your arguments, but it alone will not enable you to win the matter.

10. An attorney who undertakes litigation without goals or objectives faces an unhappy fate. The result of such stupidity is a waste of time and loss of energy.

11. Hence the saying: The enlightened ruler lays his plans well in advance, and the good general cultivates his resources.

12. No client should ever engage in litigation merely to satisfy his own emotions, and an attorney should ever fight a battle simply out of spite, anger, or resentment.

13. If it is to your advantage to make a move, then do so. If it is not to your advantage, then stay where you are.

14. Anger may in time changes to gladness; vexation may be succeeded by content.

15. But a kingdom that has once been destroyed can never come again into being; nor can the dead ever be brought back to life.

16. Hence the enlightened ruler is heedful, and the good general full of caution. This is the way to keep a country at peace and an army intact.

14. Anger in time turns to happiness, and aggravation may be followed by content.

15. But a kingdom that has been destroyed can never come back into being, nor can the dead be brought back to life.

16. Hence, the enlightened client is thoughtful, and the good attorney full of caution. This is how you keep a client at peace and your resources intact.

13
THE USE OF SPIES

Sun Tzu said:

1. Raising a host of a hundred thousand men and marching them great distances entails heavy loss on the people and a drain on the resources of the State. The daily expenditure will amount to a thousand ounces of silver. There will be commotion at home and abroad, and men will drop down exhausted on the highways. As many as seven hundred thousand families will be impeded in their labor.

2. Hostile armies may face each other for years, striving for the victory which is decided in a single day. This being so, to remain in ignorance of the enemy's condition simply because one grudges the outlay of a hundred ounces of silver in honors and emoluments, is the height of inhumanity.

3. One who acts thus is no leader of men, no present help to his sovereign, and no master of victory.

4. Thus, what enables the wise sovereign and the good general to strike and conquer, and achieve things beyond the reach of ordinary men, is foreknowledge.

5. Now this foreknowledge cannot be elicited from spirits; it cannot be obtained inductively from experience, or by any deductive calculation.

1. Sun Tzu points out that warfare is incredibly costly in human capital, resources, energy, and of course, money. Litigation can costs incredible sums of money. Conflict affects the client, the team, and their families.

2. Conflict, as is the case in litigation, can continue for many years, while victory is decided in a single day. Considering the duration and cost, it is the height of inhumanity not to know your opponent's position because of an aversion to spending a small amount of money.

3. One who acts this way is no leader, no prize to his client, and no master of victory.

4. What enables the wise client and good litigator to strike and prevail, and to achieve results beyond the reach of ordinary people, is foreknowledge.

5. This kind of foreknowledge cannot be extracted from ghosts, cannot be observed from the past, or by any empirical calculation.

6. Knowledge of the enemy's dispositions can only be obtained from other men.

7. Hence the use of spies, of whom there are five classes: (1) Local spies; (2) inward spies; (3) converted spies; (4) doomed spies; (5) surviving spies.

8. When these five kinds of spy are all at work, none can discover the secret system. This is called 'divine manipulation of the threads'. It is the sovereign's most precious faculty.

9. Having local spies means employing the services of the inhabitants of a district.

10. Having inward spies, means making use of officials of the enemy.

11. Having converted spies, means getting hold of the enemy's spies and using them for our own purposes.

12. Having doomed spies, doing certain things openly for purposes of deception, and allowing our spies to know of them and report them to the enemy.

6. Knowledge of your opponent and his position can only be obtained from people.

7. Hence, you should use witnesses to support your matter, and there are five types: 1) Lay, 2) Insiders, 3) Converted 4) Expert, 5) In-House

8. When these five kinds of witnesses are all at work, it will be difficult for your opponent to discover a secret strategy you have put in place. Sun Tzu calls it the "divine manipulation of the threads." This is your most precious resource.

9. Having Lay witnesses means obtaining people with knowledge of the facts of the matter, the character of your opponent, and its business practices.

10. Having Insiders as witnesses means obtaining people with inside knowledge of the opposing party who are willing to testify against it, such as whistleblowers or employees.

11. Converted witnesses are those who originally were supportive of your opponent, but who are now willing to testify on your client's behalf.

12. Expert witnesses are those who can provide "deceptive" information to your opponent, while bolstering your position.

13. Surviving spies, finally, are those who bring back news from the enemy's camp.

14. Hence it is that with none in the whole army are more intimate relations to be maintained than with spies. None should be more liberally rewarded. In no other business should greater secrecy be preserved.

15. Spies cannot be usefully employed without a certain intuitive sagacity.

16. They cannot be properly managed without benevolence and straightforwardness.

17. Without subtle ingenuity of mind, one cannot make certain of the truth of their reports.

18. Be subtle! Be subtle! And use your spies for every kind of business.

19. If a secret piece of news is divulged by a spy before the time is ripe, he must be put to death together with the man to whom the secret was told.

13. In-House witnesses are those who are not disclosed to your opponent, but who help you build your case, as well as your understanding of your opponent. They can include private investigators, health-care professionals, or others whom you can use in secret to evaluate your opponent's position. It can also include colleagues familiar with your opponent and your opposing counsel who can provide you information about their thought processes, styles, or other information.

14. Thus, there is no more important relationship to foster than with your witnesses. They should be kept very happy.

Further, this is the area that requires the most secrecy.

15. Witnesses cannot be usefully employed without a certain intuitive wisdom.

16. They cannot be properly managed without showing compassion while being straightforward.

17. Without the subtle ability to see below the surface, you will be unable to know whether your witnesses are being truthful with you.

18. Be subtle! Be subtle! Use your witnesses for every kind of matter.

19. If a secret piece of evidence is divulged by a witness to your opponent, you must immediately cease using and distance yourself from that witness and anyone whom the witness told.

20. Whether the object be to crush and army, to storm a city, or to assassinate an individual, it is always necessary to being by finding out the names of the attendants, the aides-de-camp, and door-keepers and sentries of the general in command. Our spies must be commissioned to ascertain these.

21. The enemy's spies who have come to spy on us must be sought out, tempted with bribes, led away and comfortably housed. Thus they will become converted spies and available to for our service.

22. It is through the information brought by the converted spy that we are able to acquire and employ local and inward spies.

23. It is owing to his information, again, that we can cause the doomed spy to carry false tiding to the enemy.

24. Lastly, it is by his information that the surviving spy can be used on appointed occasions.

25. The end and aim of spying in all its five varieties is knowledge of the enemy; and this knowledge can only be derived, in the first instance, from the converted spy. Hence it is essential that the converted spy be treated with the utmost liberality.

20. Whatever your objective in litigation, it is always necessary for you to know the names and beliefs held of all the key players and their staff, including the court. You can use your witnesses to ascertain this information.

21. You should work to convert your opponent's witnesses, using the arguments and information at your disposal to assist in this task.

22. The Converted witness can provide you information about Lay and Inside witnesses who would be helpful to your cause.

23. An Expert witness's personal background, report, and payment are how you cause a devious position to be carried to your opponent.

24. Lastly, your In-House witness should be kept secret, and disclosed or utilized only when needed.

25. Beyond using witnesses in the obvious ways, the objective of utilizing witnesses is knowledge of your opponent and his position.

The most helpful information comes from the Converted witness, which makes it essential that this person be treated with the upmost care.

26. Of old, the rise of the Yin dynasty was due to I Chih who had served under the Hsia. Likewise, the rise of the Chou dynasty was due to Lu Ya who had served under the Yin.

27. Hence it is only the enlightened ruler and the wise general who will use the highest intelligence of the army for purposes of spying and thereby they achieve great results. Spies are a most important element in warfare, because on them depends an army's ability to move.

26. In the old days, the rise of at least a couple dynasties was the result of using high-ranking officials as spies.

27. Hence, the enlightened client and wise attorney will use their smartest people to fully develop witnesses, and thereby achieve great results.

Witnesses are the most important element in a case because your position and your ability to maneuver depend on them.

The End

The following are some additional suggestions from the author which are particular to litigation and did not fit into a particular paragraph:

1. Your objective should always come first, which will probably be meeting the client's objective. Focus on that long-term goal, rather than whether or not you won or lost short-term fights.

2. Keep in mind that a win may not help meet your client's objective. You may find that you can lose a battle, but still help your client. You may shift your opponent's behavior by losing, or even box your opponent into a particular position that is helpful for you in the long run.

3. If your actions will only generate animosity, do not act unless animosity is what you seek. Similarly, be cognizant of your presentation. Don't be obtuse unless you have a specific calculated reason on a specific matter to be so. Be very careful about using the scorched earth tactics described in this book.

4. Do not risk having a mistake discovered by your opponent, because you will eventually be discovered. Own the error rather than trying to hide it. There are no secrets in life, only gaps in time before the truth is known.

5. People are not angry when they know they are winning. Thus, if your opponent personally attacks you while denigrating your position, you know that very position is

what he fears. Consider your favorite sports team when they beat a rival. The winners are on a high, not in a position where they want to physically harm the opponent's coach.

6. Remember that this book is not about obliterating your opponent; it is about learning the nature of conflict and of people.

ABOUT THE AUTHOR

Troy Doucet is an attorney who practices consumer related litigation in Columbus, Ohio. He graduated *magna cum laude* from Capital University Law School and holds his bachelor's degree in Economics from The Ohio State University. His multi-lawyer law firm is devoted to helping consumers and those facing difficulties.

Mr. Doucet published a book on litigating foreclosure cases in 2008 called *23 Legal Defenses to Foreclosure*. He also published an integrated version of Regulation Z of the Truth in Lending Act, which is now out of print.

Mr. Doucet regularly speaks about consumer litigation and can be reached through his firm's website, www.troydoucet.com.

77871414R00112

Made in the USA
Columbia, SC
28 September 2017